MW00415031

FINDING
Karishma

FINDING
Karishma

MODERN-DAY SLAVERY AND THE NEW ABOLITION MOVEMENT

ROBERT K. GOFF

A Restore International Book

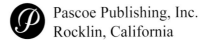

Pascoe Publishing, Inc.
Rocklin, California

Prepared in association with Edit Resource (www.editresource.com).

Cover Design by Brianna Showalter
Layout/Interior Design by Kayla Blanco

Restore International
3226 Rosedale Street, Suite 100
Gig Harbor, WA 98335.
See online at www.restoreinternational.org.

Pascoe Publishing, Inc.
www.pascoepublishing.com

ISBN: 978-1-929862-63-4
Printed in China

07   08   10   9   8   7   6   5   4   3   2   1

ACKNOWLEDGMENTS

I want to acknowledge with great appreciation the many people who played a part in the writing of this book.

What you will find within these pages is an imprint of sorts. The real authors of this book are those who pressed the wet ink of their own journeys up against the blank pages of my life in order to tell a story that I hope is worth telling. Without them and their acts of friendship, bravery, sacrifice, and faith, this book would not have been written. I am certain that I have only imperfectly assembled just part of the story that needs to be told, but I hope that for one or more people who read this book it will start a kind of internal countdown sequence that will result in their launching out into the world to make a difference for those in need.

I want to single out my bride, Maria, as well as Lindsey, Richard, and Adam Goff, who allowed me to sit in my favorite chair for months at a time with my laptop seemingly glued in place. Team Goff, you have been a constant source of inspiration and have been co-adventurers with me in every aspect of this book and the stories it contains. Thank you also to my parents.

In the writing of this book I found myself to be both a participant and a bystander.

I want to thank Eric Stanford, who labored heroically to pull together the stories and decipher what at times must have seemed an impossible amalgamation of facts, thoughts, and images. Eric, you indeed cracked the code on how to make words well and became a real friend in the process.

For all of my colleagues who have the guts and the grit to get the job done, I want to tell you how much I respect your ability to selflessly and consistently "do." Moses, Ilea, and Roberta, you are modern-day heroes as you serve so well and lead our teams in Uganda and India. Jaime Aparicio, thank you for all you have been doing in Latin America for us.

I also want to thank all of those friends who have been teaching me that it's about Jesus plus nothing else. That includes each guy in my Friday morning small group. Guys, you are my board of directors.

Restore International did not just happen. Rather, it is the bringing together of a team of gifted people who contributed their individual DNA in order to craft something that is bigger and better than any of us could have accomplished alone. I want to thank everyone who has played a part in guiding Restore International from its birth, through its infancy, and now into its adolescence. I want to acknowledge the people who have been part of the first day of operation of Restore International in the role of encouragers, friends, advisers, and "doers." In particular, I am referring to Aaron Atkinson, Nadine Vasser, Andy Miller, and Crystal Clifton as well as to the huge number of volunteers and the interns who serve at our offices. You have each played a role in everything that became a part of this book.

Musician Brandon Heath has also traveled extensively with Team Goff to India and elsewhere and has been a great friend who has encouraged me not to get comfortable.

All of our work would come to a grinding halt if it were not for Danny DeWalt, my law partner at Goff & DeWalt and second in command at Restore International. Danny, you leak Jesus as you lead and serve. Thank you for taking up the slack and for launching me.

And then I must thank our legal staff. This includes Ken Strauss, who once described his main job as giving me time, and Cynthia Niles, who is pure sunshine to all of us.

I also want to thank Tom Jonez, who is perhaps the most faithful and encouraging person I have ever met. Tom, your faith has run circles around mine. You and your family continue to show us all how to dance even in adversity. That is perhaps the greatest gift you could have given us.

Everything good about this book and the stories within it I attribute to the overwhelming goodness of the people who have stood with me every step of the way. Any shortcomings in it are entirely my own.

CONTENTS

PREFACE

To many of us in the West, slavery is an issue belonging to the past, as long gone as wooden ships plying the waters from Africa with human cargo on board. Or if we recall hearing an occasional news report about Sudanese enslaving one another, or about a Filipino woman forced into domestic servitude in the United Arab Emirates, we might have the impression that slavery at most makes isolated appearances on the world scene today. But the truth is, slavery is a far more pervasive and urgent problem than many people realize. And instances of modern-day slavery are not solely occurring in faraway places; they can and do occur in places one might think would be immune to such horrific practices.

Given the nature of forced servitude, it is impossible to document exactly how many people are suffering in such a condition today. University of Surrey professor Kevin Bales, a leading researcher in the subject, puts the number of slaves at 27 million and acknowledges that others think the total may reach as high as 200 million.[1] Even if we take the lower estimate, the number of human beings caught up in slavery today dwarfs the total number of people swept into slavery during the four hundred years of the slave trade in the New World. Slavery and other forms of human trafficking affect more men, women, and children right now than they have at any other time in history.

The breadth of the tragedy across earth's geography is one thing; the depth of the pain it causes in individuals is another. Each person making up the ranks of the enslaved is a person whose right to freedom has been stolen, whose dignity has been trampled upon, and whose future has been darkened. Whether we're talking about a man forced to work in an unsafe factory in Bolivia, a Bangladeshi family working in rice fields sunup to sundown to pay back a paltry debt, or a Thai teenager who contracts AIDS as a victim of sex tourism, we can only begin to imagine the suffering in lives that are often short and tragic. As Bales said, "Slavery is an obscenity. It is not just stealing someone's labor; it is the theft of an entire life."[2]

Finding Karishma is about modern-day slavery, especially in India. But it is about more than that. It is also about what ordinary people like you and I can do about the problem. Since much of my work in this area has been with young girls who have been sold into the brothels of India, theirs are the stories you will encounter most often in this book. But the organization I have founded, Restore International, has a larger mandate: to serve the poorest of the poor; to help end the heinous practice of human trafficking, especially the exploitation of young kids, worldwide; and in other audacious and creative ways to explore how we can launch ourselves and others to do what Jesus of Nazareth did.

How, you might ask, did a forty-six-year-old lawyer get involved in this kind of work?

***

I call myself a "recovering lawyer." What this means is that, while I have enjoyed some success in the practice of law, and indeed am still the senior partner of a law firm, I have gone on—with the support of the exceptional men and women who make up our law firm and the Restore International team—to pursue justice issues on behalf of kids who are almost invisible to most of us and who are desperately in need of an advocate.

During my career, I have had the opportunity to represent many clients, each of whom hired me to pursue a remedy that they and I considered just. But while many of these legal matters put millions of dollars into dispute, the changes that resulted from my efforts—the justice involved—were small and incremental. In other words, despite the magnitude of the transfer of wealth, the magnitude of the actual change in the lives of those participating was minimal. I wanted to be a part of something much bigger, something that would enable me to make a huge difference for victims of injustice. I found what I was searching for on a trip to India in 2002.

In India, I discovered a vast and beautiful land filled with wonderful people reflecting rich cultural influences. But I also discovered men, women, and children suffering a different kind of injustice than I was used to dealing with: I encountered India's slave trade. I visited rock quarries and brick factories where backbreaking work was performed by people who had been erroneously convinced that they had to pay off a so-called debt to the ones who had bought them. I walked into villages at night to meet with slaves who had been secretly brought there to have their cases documented in the hope of winning their freedom. I drove or walked down the streets of red-light districts and saw countless girls and young women offering their bodies for rent because they knew that if they didn't the brothel keepers and their thugs would beat them.

All of this ruined a perfectly good legal career. I concluded on the sixty-hour trip home that, while I loved the practice of law, I could not continue to practice it in a business-as-usual fashion. I decided that there was a higher calling and a better use of my skills than simply being a hired gun litigating civil matters. I could not live the same way, now that I had been exposed to a sea of needy people whose cries were no longer muffled to my Western ears. It was time for a change of trajectory, not because I didn't love practicing law, but because of the gravitational pull exerted by recognizing that I had something to contribute to ease the pain of others.

I returned home and within a week quit my then–law partnership, beginning a new practice that would allow me to follow the dictates of my conscience more closely. The current firm, Goff & DeWalt, is structured in such a way that it leaves me and my colleagues in the firm time to make a difference in the world. These talented people are really the brains of the law firm. One of the best decisions I ever made was to surround myself with people whose games are so much better than mine when it comes to loving people and serving them. I am indeed a great "picker" when it comes to people, and I have picked the best.

Now, when we win a judgment, it is not just another notch in our legal belt. Rather, we call it "fundraising." My partner, Danny DeWalt, and others in the organization volunteer some of their time and expertise to the objective of ending modern-day slavery and serving the poorest of the poor. And so, with their indispensable help on my side, pursuing justice issues for little girls is exactly what we began to do. Starting this new justice venture felt radical, irresponsible, crazy. In other words, it was a great decision!

Stepping out of my day-to-day law practice was just the beginning of my adventure. The desire to learn about and expose injustice drew me back to India again and again. With my wife's somewhat apprehensive blessing, I even took my teenage children with me to find, document, and participate in setting free kids who were just a few years older than themselves. I became smitten with the nation of India and its people, committing myself to pursuing the organized crime leaders who exploit this nation's kids. India's beauty and suffering still touch my heart every time I go there.

This commitment to India proved to be a grist mill in my life, grinding up who I used to be and spitting me out different than I was before. Because of what I saw in that land and among its people, I decided that I wanted to be more courageous than I thought I could be. To be more engaged than I ever had been. To love more than I had before—and not the hold-hands-and-walk-in-the-park kind of love, but the sort of love that will lay down a life, a career, a sense of security to gain so much more.

I decided to find and help the oppressed, not just talk about doing this. Specifically, I wanted to help kids who are without a voice in their society. From the start, I knew that I could never do it alone.

***

In my travels throughout India, I was inspired by a brave American couple who were living in Mumbai (Bombay) and who were sold out to the task of finding and releasing kids sold into brothels. Indeed, during their years in India, they had participated in the rescues of hundreds of minor girls. Like metal to a magnet, I was drawn to the eradication of child prostitution.

Through a number of discussions with people in the United States and India, Restore International was born in 2004. Our expanding staff are working primarily in India and Uganda so far. Restore's mission is not only to find and rescue young girls in brothels, but also to care for these dear ones and others with love. We do not, however, stop there; we aim to bring the perpetrators of crimes to justice. We seek to find what causes justice to be wrapped around the axle in some places and to figure out a way to fix it. While we may not be able to restore innocence to the victims, we try to restore each person's hope for the future and rain down justice on those who prey on kids and the poorest of the poor for their own selfish gain.

Our team of human rights professionals in India, Uganda, and other countries is extensive and is comprised of some of the best in the business. Restore International employs nationals in various countries possessing the array of special skills required to serve with us as investigators, attorneys, and social workers. Teams working for Restore's investigation units have been a part of numerous rescues, delivering young girls from captivity and prosecuting their captors. In India we have focused, not just on the big cities (where pressure from nongovernmental organizations has been felt already), but also in outlying areas, where the same problems exist on a massive scale because the trucking and other routes of commerce have created a huge demand for young girls in brothels.

Human rights advocacy is tricky stuff. It looks nothing like the legal practice that I had become familiar with. In our case, it involves opposing deeply entrenched practices, supported by ancient economic, tribal, and cultural traditions, and seeking justice through a system that is riddled with ineptitude and corruption. And as you will see through reading this book, while we have experienced joy beyond description, we have also suffered disappointments as well as both verbal and physical attacks at the hands of the bad guys.

Despite the challenges, at Restore International, our resolve is stronger now than ever before. We will not pretend that the problem does not exist; we will not simply hope that someone else will stand up and address it; we will not let evil prosper. We *will* find kids who are lost in sex slavery and in other ways serve the poorest of the poor.

Beyond our own efforts to redress the problem of the sexual exploitation of children, we want to bring their cries of suffering into an auditory range the world can hear. We hope that we can be a catalyst to motivate people, not merely to feel sorry for these girls and others who are disadvantaged, but to go further and *do something* about their plight. And in a broader scope, we desire to fuel a modern abolition movement that will do more than just dispense information about slavery, but that will take action as a result of a passion for justice.

The evidence that our passion is making a difference will be the formation of a corps of people who put wheels on their convictions and begin to push back the tide of human trafficking of every sort worldwide. In short, the fight needs to be brought to the bad guys. And it *can* be brought to them by people just like you and me. What we need to do first is to simply show up.

All people everywhere are meant to be free. This is not merely a catchy phrase. I believe that a yearning to be free is hardwired into us by God. It is in the DNA of people everywhere. If this is true, will we not act against this evil in our own day?

Is it a big job? Of course it is. Are the problems going to go away easily? Of course they won't. Let's not be satisfied, however, just to do what we think we can, but let's do what we ought to do. Let's not just feel others' pain, but let's reach in and become a part of their release. And let's not be satisfied with being compassionate bystanders, but let's be engaged liberators. By doing so, we can confront this global issue of injustice against kids and grown-ups alike.

This book presents many stories involving investigators, informants, and others in India (and sometimes elsewhere) with whom we work or have worked. In each case, we have changed their names so that their security will not be compromised. After all, they are still out there in the field, infiltrating brothels, organizing rescue operations, and prosecuting the perpetrators with us or other organizations. Similarly, we have changed the names of victims in order to respect their privacy. This being said, though, let me assure you that all the stories contained in this book are 100 percent real.

And now let me introduce to you a young girl whose circumstances illustrate the suffering and misery that are among the terrible costs associated with the flesh trade. Her name is Karishma…

PART ONE:

Slavery Today

ONE

The One Who Got Away

Karishma and the Tragedy of Child Slavery

In the steamy hotel room in Miraj, India, where I had spent the evening anxiously awaiting the return of our investigator, Pranit Mayakunar, I watched the footage he brought back on his covert camera, and my heart was wrung with what I saw.

The man with the tiny video camera hidden in his shirt pocket, thirty-one-year-old Pranit, was posing as a brothel customer with a penchant for young girls. In the video I could see that the brothel keeper whom Pranit had contacted was an overweight woman who looked to be in her sixties, with a large nose and a bindi spot between her eyebrows, wearing a pink and blue sari. She entered a narrow room with whitewashed walls and stick rafters, lit by a single hanging light bulb. As Pranit waited by the door, the woman walked to a bed at the back of the room, partially hidden by a hanging curtain, and there she flung back the tattered brown blanket that was draped over a metal-frame bed.

Curled up underneath was an angry girl who was barely twelve years old. She was thin, pretty, with her hair caught up in a disorderly ponytail, and she was wearing a dirty and crumpled Western-style dress. The girl knew what the older woman had come to tell her—that there was another customer waiting to rape her, and she had better get up and cooperate. The words passing between the two were inaudible on the footage, but the gestures exchanged made the audio unnecessary. It was plain that the girl was arguing, gesturing violently, and turning her face to the wall. At one point the girl threw the covers over her head again in protest at what she was being ordered once again to do. Like a scavenger wolf, repeatedly the fat brothel keeper poked and prodded until the little girl stood up angrily, pushed the older woman away, and finally leaned against a wall in the shadows, defeated and momentarily isolated from her keeper. She couldn't have been more than four and a half feet tall.

The video went on to document the transaction by which Pranit bought the right to rape this child. In order to approach the girl, he had to step over some people sleeping on the floor—an old lady and another young child who seemed to be lying almost lifeless on the dirty floor at the time. But once he did that, he handed the agreed-upon fee of one hundred rupees (a little more than $2.00) over to the girl, and she immediately turned the entire amount over to her brothel keeper. Then the keeper ushered them both into the room next door.

With its dirt floor and whitewashed walls, this room looked much like the first one, except that the two of them were alone in there. It was furnished solely with a metal-frame bed and a bucket for receiving used condoms. The girl sat down on the bed with resignation, but instead of what she expected to happen, the man began to talk.

This was not his first time there. Pranit had come to visit this girl for the last two nights in a row, both times never touching her, but only asking her to talk about herself. And this time he was back with the video camera running and said that once again he only wanted to talk, and he started asking questions about her. As the girl spoke fitfully about her life, she remained upset, at times crying, looking dazed, and flopping back on the bed in exhaustion. Nevertheless, as they talked, Pranit managed to get a partial profile of the girl's situation: her name was Karishma, she was from the nearby state of Karnataka, and she was new to prostitution. She also mentioned that the local police had been among her customers. After learning these details, Pranit sat next to Karishma, gently told her that he would return tomorrow, and urged her to get some rest.

The video came to an end with Pranit leaving the building. As I sat there in my hotel room, I knew that I would never forget the look I had seen on Karishma's face when she was faced with the prospect of being raped once again. It was a look of anger, of despair, of pain. It was the look of a girl who ought to have been going to school and enjoying an innocent youth, but who instead was trapped and miserable in a life no one, young or old, should have to endure. And it was a look that reminded me more plainly than any amount of statistics or any dry recitation of facts could do about why I was in India.

This image of a distraught Karishma in her brothel was taken with a hidden video camera by Restore International investigator Pranit Mayakunar.

Finding Karishma—the First Time

I am the founder of Restore International, a nongovernmental organization focused upon serving the poorest of the poor and rescuing children who are exploited under slavery or slavery-like conditions. One of our chief goals is to rescue some of the hundreds of thousands of underage girls who have been put to work in the brothels of India and in other countries against their will and against the laws of those lands. With the help of investigators like Pranit, we find them and pull them out one by one.

The investigation that uncovered the presence of Karishma in the red-light district of Miraj, leading up to Pranit's videotaping of Karishma in the early evening of October 17, 2005, was much like our other investigations. Restore's India operations chief and I, along with our team of Indian investigators, had been in the area for some days. Specifically, we had been in the nearby town of Sangli, following up a previous rescue operation. Bad news travels fast, and the bad news that day was that Restore's people had arrived in Sangli once again.

In an attempt to maintain a low profile, we had gone into the basement area of a local restaurant for a quick meal after a long drive. Within minutes, we noticed that we had been flanked by men who had ordered meals but, who seemed only to have an interest in leveling piercing stares at us while they attempted to eavesdrop on our conversation. It didn't take long to figure out that they were probably associated with the brothel owners and pimps who had been the subject of a previous raid we had conducted with the police in the area.

When we finished our meal, we decided that we would have the investigators whom we had brought leave apart from us in order to keep their cover intact. It turned out to be a wise decision, because as we emerged from the basement area of the restaurant where we had eaten, we were immediately confronted by some brothel keepers from the Gokul Nagar red-light area and their thugs. It was then that we decided it would be prudent to shift our operations for the next few evenings to Sangli's sister city of Miraj.

Located not quite two hundred miles southeast of Mumbai (Bombay) in Maharashtra State, Miraj has a population of around 125,000 persons. Its red-light district, called Prem Nagar, while not as large as the one in Sangli, is extensive (about the size of a football field) for a city of its population. One reason for this is that Miraj sits at a crossroads of India's highways, and large numbers of truck drivers park their rigs at the Miraj truck stop and make their way the few hundred yards to Prem Nagar in order to make use of the prostitutes who line the streets there.

Despite the opposition we had run up against in Sangli, we were confident that we were as yet unknown in Miraj, and so we rented rooms in a hotel that was literally right next to the Prem Nagar red-light area and started our investigations. On the first night, we headed into Prem Nagar at around seven o'clock in the evening. The safest way to perform reconnaissance of an area like this is to hail an auto rickshaw, which is a three-wheeled cab powered by a small motorcycle engine. On that night, the fumes and racket from our rickshaw made it almost impossible to sit in the bench seat in back without choking. However, the configuration of the cab allowed us to navigate the narrow roads while staying in the shadows and avoiding too much attention from the scores of brothel owners and prostitutes lining the streets. In addition to this reconnaissance, we had our investigators walking up and down the streets, attempting with us to identify girls who appeared to be under the age of eighteen.

Entering the red-light district, we all immediately experienced an oppressive feeling. In part, this was because of the spirit of vice and evil that filled the place. And in part it was because the road into the brothel district had no streetlights, leaving the area in darkness save for the shadowy figures who were sprinkled along both sides of the roads and who were for sale. The only lighting came from a few kerosene lamps behind the bars of some of the glassless windows in the brothels. The air was filled with a heavy smell of exhaust from the motor rickshaws that carried customers into and out of the area. The only competing smells were the fumes from the diesel trucks idling at the nearby truck stop and the odors of burning wood and cooking fires.

Brothels lined both sides of the main road as well as the cross streets. Most of the brothels were whitewashed and nondescript. A few were decorated with some stripes or color, though at night they were barely distinguishable from one another. All of them were dark and dirty places. Many had no doors, only open doorways revealing glimpses of more shadowy inhabitants inside. In the monsoon season these shabby brothels would smell musty and for the rest of the year they would remain hot and stuffy. When it comes to this type of oppression, however, there are no seasons.

It was early in the evening for the sex trade, but there were a number of other customers (as our investigators were pretending to be) walking up and down the streets. Meanwhile, pimps and prostitutes were scattered along each side of the road. Some of the prostitutes, particularly the younger ones, were standing, while the older ones sat on the ground in groups of from three to five, quietly talking. I wondered what these women would be talking about in this dark and dank place. The reason they were there was clear. They were advertising their wares for sale as if the street were a large and windowless shop. It is a buyer's market in such places, and the customers take their time in making their pick. Even then, a negotiation about price and bargain hunting might result in still further tire-kicking without a purchase.

Early on, we identified three or four girls who appeared to be underage. Mentally, we targeted these girls for closer investigation—they were the reason why we were there. Sadly, however, we were not able to get close to the one girl who looked to be the youngest.

This little girl had been seen by our investigators underneath a bridge with her keeper watching over her. Our Indian investigators, Pranit and another man named Mohal, were sent in a rickshaw to act as customers interested in this girl. Mohal remained in the rickshaw while Pranit approached the pimp and started negotiating for the girl's services.

India is often referred to as the land of a thousand languages. This is a conservative estimate. Even areas separated by small distances carry distinctive language differences. Because the rickshaw operators are closely connected with the brothel owners in the area, those with accents remote to the area are immediately suspect by them in the red-light areas.

Our investigators were successful in weaving together a story about why they had arrived in the area. Apparently, however, the girl's keeper was being extra cautious due to the extreme young age of his victim. When he noticed that Pranit had an accent proving that he was from a different part of India, he got suspicious and sent Pranit away. Who knows what eventually became of this girl?

Of the other underage girls we identified, one was Karishma. She was barely twelve years old. We first spotted her standing beside the road, as she was forced to do when not servicing a customer. Young girls are often sent out on the street in order to lure men into the brothels to take a look at the other women and girls inside. Pedophiles are plentiful in these areas. Perverted lust is not the only reason that young girls are sought after; with the widespread nature of the AIDS epidemic in India now rivaling and soon expected to surpass that of South Africa, young girls are sought in the hopes that they are not carriers of the virus.

We knew from our prior experience with red-light districts like this one that young girls such as Karishma are required to submit to as many as fifteen to twenty men each day, keeping little or none of the money they earn for themselves. We also knew that, if *we* could spot her so easily, then surely the local police must also know of her presence and were doing nothing about it.[1] Unfortunately, we would learn from Karishma herself later that the police who were supposed to be protecting her were in fact her tormentors and customers on a regular basis.

We quickly laid plans for Pranit to try to get enough evidence so that we could force the police into rescuing this girl. Still posing as a customer, and working his way through a maze of darkened entrances, Pranit got access to the brothel where Karishma was held. The brothel was set back from the street by twenty yards and was reached by going through an unlit space between two shacks. The brothel was dark, filthy, and populated not only by the brothel keeper, but also by some young children and an old woman in her eighties.

That first night, Pranit paid the going rate of about one hundred rupees—the price of a soda pop in most places. With Karishma, he was led by the brothel owner to the room next door where customers were entertained. He used the ruse common for the investigators to explain why they would simply sit with the victims, saying to Karishma, "I'm not in the mood right now. I've just broken up with my girlfriend. Can we just talk?"

Usually the investigators get just one shot using this approach, since the girls become suspicious if they use it more than once. Fortunately that was not true with Karishma, as Pranit had to go back three times over the course of two nights to get enough information for us to act upon. Perhaps because she was so new to the business Karishma didn't think much of the fact that this young man paid to spend time with her three times, but never had sex with her.

Finally, by the third night, Pranit managed to get footage of a distraught Karishma that was both compelling and unequivocal. Our team sat together back at the hotel room riveted to the scenes that required no narration as Karishma attempted to fight off the brothel owner's bantering as she forced Karishma to her feet from under a blanket where she had been hiding. The mood was somber. No one could speak. We knew, though, that we would do whatever it would take to see Karishma free from the misery she was trapped in.

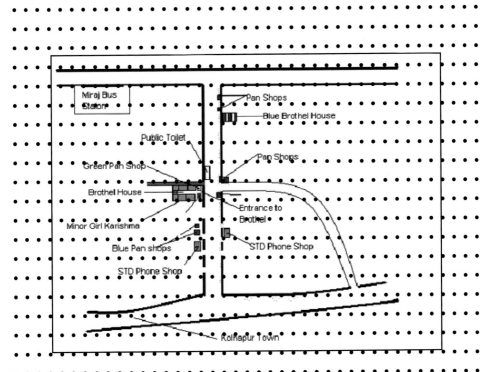

The map we gave to the Miraj police to show them where Karishma was being held in the Prem Nagar red-light district.

What It Took to Get a Raid

Pranit's video was valuable evidence. It proved beyond a doubt that a twelve-year-old girl was being prostituted against her will—a crime under Indian law. We knew that getting the local police to enforce the law might be difficult, even with this evidence, but we had to try.

The next morning, we arrived at the Miraj police headquarters just as the deputy superintendent of police, Digambar Pradhan, was getting into his car to attend the funeral of a former Member of Parliament from the area who had recently died. We stopped him and told him that we had video footage of a minor girl in the Prem Nagar red-light district of Miraj.

At this he got out of his car and asked, "How long will it take to set up the video projection?"

We replied, "We have it right here." We had already queued up the tape on one of our undercover recording decks, and we played it for the superintendent immediately.

Superintendent Pradhan watched the tape through to its end. After it was over, he made no comment about what he'd seen, only saying, "I'll look into it."

We handed him a map that depicted precisely where Karishma could be found amid the warren of shabby buildings that made up the red-light district. Then Pradhan nodded and left for the funeral.

We waited throughout the day, hoping to hear that the police wanted us to be a part of a raid upon Prem Nagar. As it turned out, Pranit was unable to fulfill his promise, effectively made to Karishma, to return that day as part of a rescue operation. When we checked repeatedly with the police, they remained unwilling to do anything about Karishma or any of the other enslaved child prostitutes in their community, giving all sorts of excuses for why they would not act.

The next day and the next, we repeated our request for a raid, and each time we were refused. Hand-delivered letters were no more successful in moving the deputy superintendent to act. And then, unfortunately, another investigation we were engaged in at the time went awry (a story told in chapter five) and, with our cover blown, the Restore team was forced to leave the area. It broke my heart to go away while Karishma was still being held in captivity. But we had no intention of giving up.

Around three weeks after our original investigation into Karishma's captivity, in response to the continued phone calls and letters of our people on the ground, we finally got a verbal agreement from the Miraj police to conduct a raid at Prem Nagar. So we quickly sent another team to Miraj and used a new investigator to verify that Karishma was still being held in the brothel. She was. However, even after having given us an assurance that they would conduct a raid, incredibly, once again the police still did nothing.

Finally, following three more days of barraging the deputy superintendent with letters and in-person requests for a raid—all to no avail—our people decided to go over the head of the local police. Driving two hours to the larger city of Kolhapur, our team spoke to the chief of police there about Karishma's plight. This man was much more responsive and immediately ordered the Miraj police superintendent, his subordinate, to conduct a raid of the brothel.

At last we were going to get some action.

Karishma's Story

On the morning after he had traveled to Kolhapur, one of our people had the opportunity to meet with a local church leader and an associate of his. These men, both deeply involved in social service, had already expressed an interest in the work Restore was doing with young girls trapped in prostitution. When the reverend was shown the videotape of Karishma, before long he leaned forward to get a better look at the face of the girl on the tape and declared, "That's Kamutchi!"

To the great surprise of our people, it turned out that both the reverend and his friend knew the girl we were about to try to rescue. Along with Karishma—the name she had called herself—Kamutchi was another nickname for this girl, whose actual name was Kusumavati.

The two men were able to fill our people in on some of Karishma's background. She was twelve years old and the daughter of a prostitute who had worked in the Sangli-Miraj area. When her mother became ill with AIDS, Karishma came into the care of the home for needy children that the reverend operated. He had even helped admit her to school in the village of Digrej outside of Sangli.

Karishma was a troubled child and she ran away from this home three times. The first two times, the reverend went to the red-light district where her mother worked and retrieved her. By the third time when the reverend went to get her, Karishma's mother had died. Karishma was now under the control of the woman we saw in the video. With the death of Karishma's mother, the brothel keeper had no one else to support her. The answer for the brothel keeper was simple. She put Karishma to work as a prostitute in her mother's place.

While what we had learned was tremendously sad, there was nothing surprising in it. The children of prostitutes are some of the most vulnerable to sex trafficking, and it was almost inevitable that Karishma would end up in the flesh trade so long as she stayed in Prem Nagar.[2] The reverend had to go home without the young girl that night, and Karishma was left to unwillingly ply her awful trade. Unless, of course, someone could get her out of her captivity.

Losing Karishma

Learning Karishma's true name and story—and seeing how close she had been to having a normal life for a young girl in the region—made all of us that much more eager to convince the police to rescue her. We had our people go back to the Miraj police station one more time and begged the officers to go in and raid the brothel. Having received their orders from the superior in Kolhapur, they at last agreed to conduct a raid that very day. At one o'clock in the afternoon of November 22, 2005, a team of police and Restore International staff persons showed up at Karishma's brothel.

She wasn't there.

Clearly the brothel keeper had been tipped off by the police that a raid was coming, and so she had spirited Karishma away to someplace else. That's why the corrupt police had been willing to do the raid on this day; they knew that the brothel owner had been warned and their quarry was gone. The brothel keeper gave the story that Karishma had left a couple of days previously and would return soon. In front of the Restore team, the police made a show of demanding that the brothel keeper produce Karishma as soon as she returned "or else." And so the staged event ended. The "or else" never happened.

It was a tremendous letdown for us, especially since we had just that day finally gotten to know further details about who this precious little girl was. We kept in touch with the police in case Karishma returned, which we thought was possible because the brothel was the only "home" Karishma knew and her brothel keeper was the only "family" she had, but she didn't come back. We sent our investigators to the village where she had originally come from, thinking she might have shown up there, but no one in the village knew anything about her. Months passed, and the trail went cold.

Where is Karishma now? we wondered. Possibly in order to avoid the police, who had at least exerted nominal pressure on the brothel owner, she was being hidden in some remote village, and in that case she might be relatively safe for now. Sadly, though, we knew that it was far more likely she was being abused in the same way as before in a different red-light district in some neighboring state in India. After all, she was a proven moneymaker for people with no scruples. So what if she was a human being with a right to live her own life? So what if she had a better than 50 percent chance of dying of AIDS like her mother? She was considered property.

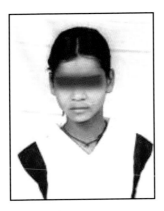

This photo of Karishma was taken during her enrollment in a village school, shortly before she came under the control of a brothel keeper. This is how she ought to look—a normal Indian schoolgirl, not a victim of men's lust.

Miracle Child

In Hindi, the name Karishma means "miracle." At this point, it seemed to us that finding her would be a miracle—not impossible, but not likely. She had disappeared into the hordes of low-cost child prostitutes flooding the streets of India's red-light areas under coercion to enrich others in the moral underbelly of the nation. In other words, she was just another one of many young victims.

This all made me struggle for a sense of compass heading in a country that widely accepts and allows the immoral practice of child prostitution. *Where do we start?* I wondered. I reflected on the model left by Jesus of Nazareth in which he was interested in "the one," not in big numbers. This principle had a galvanizing effect on every person working for Restore International and they became committed from top to bottom to finding "the one." So we never forgot Karishma, nor did we give up trying to find her. We continued to press the Indian police to locate her, even while we continued to conduct our own investigations based upon the limited leads we still had.

Why did we care so much about this one girl? Because, for all of us, Karishma had become the face of the massive victimization caused by trafficking in persons in India and elsewhere around the world. And also because the abuse and enslavement of even one girl merits the outrage of any morally healthy person. If Jesus's parable about a shepherd searching for the one lost sheep out of a hundred is to be believed, the "Father in heaven is not willing that any of these little ones should be lost."[3] Similarly, at Restore International, we recognize our own limitations, but we also recognize that we had something that we could contribute to the fight. We could keep trying to find Karishma.

Does it matter that one child is released from a brothel? That a handful are rescued in a police raid we instigate? That over the course of a year some hundreds are rescued by various NGOs in India out of the hundreds of thousands in captivity? We believe so. Each and every one matters. And so we decided that we will not rest until the Karishmas of the world are accorded the dignity they deserve and are released into the liberty that is their birthright.

Sadly but truly, it is not just one person in this world, or even a few, who wake up every morning knowing their life is not their own. *Millions* of people around the world, men, women, and children, in the supposedly enlightened twenty-first century, are victims of all kinds of slavery. Do the rest of us understand what is happening to them? Will we do anything about it?

I have learned, both in advocacy and in life, that sometimes it is not just asking questions that matter; it's being a part of the answer.

TWO
For Sale: Human Beings

Slavery in the Twenty-First Century

The night was sweltering hot and velvety black. I was in rural India walking up a dirt trail from the road where the group I was with had left our transportation to reach a village hidden by trees. In the darkness on each side of the trail I spied the weird, shadowy shapes made by anthills that reached to as much as six feet in height. My Indian friend, Mohal, informed me that each anthill was riddled with hundreds of holes that housed many different kinds of creatures, including deadly cobras. This information added to the unease I was already feeling.

It was March 2002, and I was with a team of human rights workers with an outstanding human rights organization, the International Justice Mission, who had come to Tamil Nadu to meet secretly with bonded laborers—men and women who had pledged themselves against a loan of money. These were practices strictly outlawed in India. Yet some of these young men and women were working to pay back a "debt" of as little as two hundred rupees (around four U.S. dollars). And these uneducated, illiterate people had little conception of how much their labor was truly worth or of how long it should take, at a reasonable rate, to pay back such a debt. Further, the slave traders would require that the entire so-called debt be paid in one lump sum and sometimes at interest rates of hundreds of percent. Just as the greyhounds never catch the rabbit in a dog race, so resolution of their "debt" usually stays just out of reach of the bonded laborers.

Among the debt bondage victims I encountered, some were forced to work at backbreaking jobs such as rock quarrying, farming, or rolling *beedi* cigarettes sometimes seven days a week, twelve hours a day. This would continue for years or even for the rest of their lives to pay back their "debt." In short, their debt repayment was a fiction and, functionally speaking, they were merely modern-day slaves. The chains were economic ones, but the cruelty of the *mudalalis* (slave owners) who "owned" them was as real as it gets.

Debt bondage is a widespread practice in South Asia and surrounding areas. There are estimated to be as many as 20 million bonded laborers working in India, Pakistan, Bangladesh, and Nepal, which together make up a large percentage of the world's total number of modern-day slaves.[1] This ancient evil continues to victimize the poorest of the poor even though it has been outlawed in India since 1976.[2] On the night I threaded my way through the cobra-infested anthills, my goal, and that of my companions, was to document the plight of bonded laborers in this area so that we could seek to have them removed from their mudalalis in accordance with Indian law.[3]

When we reached the remote village northeast of Tiruvanantapuram, we headed toward a common-looking building—made of whitewashed walls and a concrete floor—that doubled as a church and central meeting place for the villagers. On this particular night, while most of the villagers slept, the church was lit up with one or two bare light bulbs hung from the ceiling. When we arrived, the walls of the building were almost completely obscured by a huge crowd of bonded slaves who had made their way to the humble building in the hopes of finding freedom.

Heading in through the side door, I was struck by the presence of two five-gallon metal pots on the floor, each half filled with rice. When I asked about these pots, I was informed by one of the locals that this is where the villagers make tithe offerings. A handful of rice would be put in by those with enough, and a handful could be taken out by those who needed more. The contrast struck me as stark, as this generosity represented the best in Indian nature, while the slaveholding and debt bondage that we were there to interdict represented the worst.

Out in front of the church more of the slaves were already waiting, having been brought to the village without the knowledge of the slave traders who "owned" them. The team and I, with the help of interpreters who spoke the local Tamil language, invited them into the building, as room would permit, and we began documenting their stories. "What is your name?" we asked. "How old are you? Where are you from? Who is your mudalali?

When and how did you come into his service? Is there a debt that you must pay before you are free to leave? How does he treat you? Have you been injured by your mudalali when he is unhappy with your work?" Each of the elements of the statutes prohibiting this slave practice were addressed in our questions.

I quickly learned that beating, burning, and withholding food or water from bonded laborers were commonplace practices for mudalalis. In addition, some of the slaves revealed to us their scars as evidence of the abuse of power and the viciousness shown by their mudalalis and the thugs hired by the mudalalis to keep order. We photo-documented the injuries for the purpose of securing the release of each of the slaves. It was quickly becoming obvious to me that the real poisonous snakes in these parts were the mudalalis.

Suddenly a palpable sense of worry swept through the villagers and those waiting to meet with us. Word came that the mudalalis had discovered that the slaves were missing and had found out what we were doing. According to the rumors, the mudalalis' thugs were even then on the way to the village to deal with us in their fashion and to haul the slaves back. We couldn't be sure the rumors were true, but neither could we take a chance on it, and so we quickly broke up our operations and made plans to meet at another location. We left in the black of night along the same narrow path by which we had come to the village.

Before we got far, however, a message was passed to us that a pastor in the nearby village had volunteered to let the slaves meet with us at his home. This offer was not without risk in a small village where accounts could be settled at a later date and examples could be made of those lacking in power. However, the courageous pastor understood the importance of our work, and so he was willing to assume the risk. We eagerly took him up on his offer so that we could finish getting the evidentiary basis we needed to help free these enslaved people.

Word about the change of venue passed to the slaves, and when we arrived at the pastor's house, there were perhaps thirty slaves already there. The slaves, however, kept coming. In fact, soon so many slaves had arrived to tell their stories, in the hopes of being set free, that the only place left to meet with them was on the flat roof of the pastor's humble brick house. At one point there were as many as fifty slaves sitting on the roof with us, resembling a scene that seemed more in context someplace in the ancient world of the Bible, where one man might be lowered through the roof to be healed. I remember wondering at the time if the roof would at any moment let go under the weight of the people and we would all be abruptly lowered into the house.

Having resumed our work well after midnight this time, we continued throughout the night documenting the slaves' vital facts, fingerprinting them, and listening as they told us about the abuse they had been subjected to. Finally, the last of the slaves headed home so they would not be caught missing when the day's work started. I remember lying in bed that night and being moved to tears at the experience of the previous twenty hours and the magnitude of the human suffering represented.

The next day we traveled to a nearby city to meet with the district collector. (The job of a district collector is a holdover from the British colonial times when a collector was given the responsibility to collect taxes and oversee other civil duties. The district collector is one of the most powerful governmental officials of the district and, among other things, is in charge of law and order.) Our purpose was to present the case of the documented bonded laborers who had been sold into a life of slavery in violation of the laws of their country. I was in touch with the fact that, for perhaps the first time in their lives, these poor souls had a voice and a shot at freedom. With a great deal of joy, I learned later that as a result of the reports and action initiated by the district collector, these bonded laborers whom we had documented and advocated for were freed.

There would be many other midnight meetings in other unlikely places to document the plight of bonded laborers. I even returned later with a couple of my own children to have them help me document the facts about some of these laborers. Watching Lindsey and Richard (then eleven and thirteen, respectively) photograph, fingerprint, and write down the stories of young people only a few years old than themselves who were being held as slaves in a cave behind mudalali Gopal's house was compelling to me. I thought, *What better experience could they have in doing the things that Jesus did than to be a part of setting kids who were little older than they were free from a life of slavery?* Since then, not only Lindsey and Richard, but also their younger brother, Adam, have traveled overseas with me to take part in hands-on justice work. Seeing in my children's faces the satisfaction that came when their efforts led to police freeing captive people reminded me again that what we need to do, regardless of our age, is just to show up. And when we do, wedding faith and action together, we each can make differences that can change the trajectory of another person's life.

Indeed, I have learned that it's all about trajectory as I advocate for eradicating, not only bonded labor and the kind of prostitution into which

Karishma had been forced, but also other forms of slavery still practiced throughout the world today. The trajectory change that has been the greatest, however, has been the one in my own life as I have moved from talking about doing something to actually doing it.

Slavery by Any Name

Slavery seems like an anachronism, as out of place in the twenty-first century as top hats and petticoats. *Doesn't slavery belong to the past?* we might wonder. No, it has not only survived, but it is thriving, having adapted handily to our modern global economy. Criminalized, it has slipped into the shadows, yet every one of us reaps some of its benefits by buying inexpensive goods made by slave labor, and every one of us pays some of its costs by handing over our tax dollars to fight this scourge. Slavery is not only alive and well; it's got its grimy hands all over us. So we'd better take note of this evil that is casting one of the darkest shadows across human civilization.

In addition to the word *slavery*, terms such as *human trafficking, forced labor,* and *servitude* are used to describe what amounts to slavery.[4] And choosing the terminology is just the start of complications when we begin looking closely at this phenomenon. How, exactly, should we define modern-day slavery? National and international bodies have tried for years to encapsulate the practice in verbal descriptions.[5] Possibly the simplest and most useful definition is the one offered by University of Surrey professor Kevin Bales when he says, "Slavery is a state marked by the loss of free will, in which a person is forced through violence or the threat of violence to give up the ability to sell freely his or her own labor power." Bales goes on to enumerate, "In this definition, slavery has three key dimensions: loss of free will, the appropriation of labor power, and the use or threat of violence."[6] When all three are present, he says, you have slavery.

Problems of labeling and defining slavery are closely related to the question of how many people are enslaved today. The UN-affiliated International Labor Organization (ILO) conservatively estimates that 12.3 million persons worldwide are victims of what it calls "forced labour."[7] The U.S. State Department estimates that from six hundred thousand to eight hundred thousand persons are trafficked across national borders each year, but it does not attempt to estimate the number of people trafficked within their own nations, instead choosing to cite the ILO figure of 12.3 million.[8] Meanwhile, Kevin Bales, following his three-dimension definition

Victim Profile:
Silvia,
a Domestic Slave

Silvia was a young, single Sri Lankan mother seeking a better life for herself and her three-year-old son when she answered an advertisement for a housekeeping job in Lebanon. In the Beirut job agency, her passport was taken and she was hired by a Lebanese woman who subsequently confined her and restricted her access to food and communications. Treated like a prisoner and beaten daily, Silvia was determined to escape. She jumped from a window to the street below, landing with such force that she is permanently paralyzed. She is now back in Sri Lanka. Today she travels around the country telling her story so that others do not suffer a similar fate.[12]

of slavery and using his own research principles, estimates that there are 27 million persons enslaved worldwide. He also mentions that others have thrown out estimates ranging as high as 200 million.[9]

All who have attempted to calculate the number of slaves in the world point out how difficult it is to come up with a reliable number. Social researchers rely upon such instruments as regional surveys, law enforcement studies, and voluntary reporting by governments, along with careful extrapolation, to arrive at their estimates. Since slavery has come to be widely criminalized, it has gone underground, where it is harder to both identify and quantify. At the same time, governments have a vested interest in downplaying the presence of slavery within their own nations, and so they may underreport their slaves.[10] Still, it is beyond question that the true number of slaves must reach to the tens if not hundreds of millions.

To get an idea of how large a problem we're looking at, realize that about 13 million slaves were shipped from Africa during the entire period of the trans-Atlantic slave trade. That's less than half of the widely quoted estimate of 27 million slaves who exist right now, as you read this book. As a percentage of the world population, the slave population is no doubt smaller now than it was in earlier times. Due to the worldwide population explosion, the actual number of slaves is far greater than ever before, and it appears to be growing.[11] In one sense, though, all the estimates and comparisons are beside the point, for whether the actual number of slaves is 12 million, 27 million, or 200 million, it is far too high. The theft of freedom from even one person is an outrage.

The New Slavery—Like the Old Except Worse

While slavery has not gone away, it *has* changed. Arguably, in fact, it has gotten worse since the days when African slaves picked cotton on American plantations.

One major change in slavery is that it is no longer legal. In the pre–Civil War American South, or indeed for millennia earlier and in every part of the globe, some persons were within their rights, as the law then existed, in owning others.[13] If there was any controversy at all attached to slavery—and often there was not—it was about whether slavery was moral, not about whether it was legal. There was a consensus (among the free people, anyway) that human beings could be considered chattel, or wholly owned property, of other human beings. Sometimes ex-slaves even went on, after receiving their freedom, to own other slaves. As proof that the human race can change, the rare cries for abolition that were raised throughout the early ages of history at last multiplied and reached a crescendo when a majority of people in most parts of the world were willing to condemn slavery.

The movement for the abolition of slavery peaked in the nineteenth century. Through the efforts of activists like William Wilberforce, Britain's Parliament passed a comprehensive measure abolishing the slave trade in 1807 and then made into law the Emancipation Act of 1833 to set free the slaves held within British possessions. In the United States, Abraham Lincoln's Emancipation Proclamation of 1863 declared free the slaves who were held in Confederate areas, with the Thirteenth Amendment to the Constitution freeing all remaining American slaves in 1865. Other nations outlawed slaveholding at different times during the century, including France in 1848, Spain in 1886, and Brazil in 1888.

In the twentieth century, when international governing bodies were formed, these institutions also said no to slavery. In 1926 the League of Nations adopted the Slavery, Servitude, Forced Labor and Similar Institutions and Practices Convention. The United Nations enhanced the Slavery Convention of 1926 exactly thirty years later when it adopted the still more wordily named Supplementary Convention on the Abolition of Slavery, the Slave Trade, and Institutions and Practices Similar to Slavery. Already, in 1948, the UN had adopted the Universal Declaration of Human Rights, whose fourth article prohibits all forms of slavery and the slave trade. The Universal Declaration was given legal clout in 1966 when the UN adopted two binding covenants: the International Covenant on Economic, Social and Cultural Rights and the International Covenant on Civil and Political Rights.[14]

While slavery now contravenes national and international law, many have chosen to continue practicing it when it is in their economic favor to do so. In few cases does anyone today actually own another person, but in a great many cases—as we have seen, perhaps 27 million cases or more—people use force or the threat of force to expropriate the labor of others. In the words of Kevin Bales, "When people buy slaves today they don't ask for a receipt or ownership papers, but they do gain *control*—and they use violence to maintain this control. Slaveholders have all of the benefits of ownership without the legalities. Indeed, for the slaveholders, not having legal ownership is an improvement because they get total control without any responsibility for what they own."[15]

Bad is never good, and wrong is never right, regardless of the laws at the time. However, the history and the conditions of slavery have varied considerably from place to place and from age to age. Amid all that variety, history reports a number of examples of slaves being treated relatively well. In ancient Babylonia and Rome, for example, slaves served as soldiers, business agents, and senior administrators. In the 1820s, black slave herdsmen in the British Cape Colony were allowed to tend herds of livestock in regions so remote that they would go weeks without sighting a white figure of authority. In the 1850s an American slave named Simon Gray served as the captain of a flatboat on the Mississippi River, managing a crew that included white men.[16] No doubt these represent the best examples in the history of slavery, with an absence of the cruelty, mistreatment, deprivation, and even murder that were otherwise common. Even under the best conditions, however, captivity is captivity.

My point is that when slavery was legal, there tended to be requirements or at least expectations for how slaveholders should treat their slaves—responsibilities as well as rights. Nowadays, however, with slavery criminalized, there are no binding sanctions to hold slaveholders accountable for their treatment of those within their power. If they don't get caught, slaveholders can do whatever they want with their slaves.

Changes in world economic realities have reinforced this change for the worse in the character of slavery. Population growth ensures that there are literally millions of people in poor areas who are young, desperate, and vulnerable. Meanwhile, the globalization of the economy has disrupted the traditional subsistence trades that once provided security and has created a situation in which competition is driving down labor costs in many areas. What all this means is that, while slaves were once expensive investments for their owners, now they are perceived as cheap, throwaway resources.

The unscrupulous can snatch up the vulnerable, squeeze as much profit out of them as they can by whatever means it takes, and discard them when they are no longer profitable (perhaps after just a few years or even months, though it may be much longer). After all, there are always more potential slaves at hand.

In such an environment, we can note another difference between the old slavery and the new: slavery today is not about race. While differences of race or ethnicity, caste, and religion can play a part in certain manifestations of slavery around the world, slavery is really about the powerful taking advantage of the powerless. Vulnerability is the common denominator among slaves. Those with less money, less education, less social status, fewer political rights, weaker physical strength—these are the poorest of the poor and the ones upon whom traffickers prey.

It is not surprising, then, that while people of all ages and both genders may be trafficked, the young and females are most likely to suffer this treatment. The U.S. State Department has determined that 80 percent of those trafficked internationally are women and girls and that 50 percent are minors.[17] Meanwhile, the ILO says that of those subjected to forced economic exploitation, 56 percent are women and girls. When it comes to forced commercial sexual exploitation, the gender disparity is far greater: 98 percent of the victims are women and girls. The ILO further estimates that from 40 to 50 percent of all victims are minors.[18]

Where the Slaves Are

Almost every country in the world admits the blot of slavery. Even in the United States an estimated eighteen to twenty thousand persons

---

Inside the Mind of a Slaveholder

The following open admission by a slaveholder in India reveals the social prejudice, power imbalance, and paternalism common to much modern-day slavery.

Of course I have bonded laborers: I'm a landlord. I keep them and their families, and they work for me. When they aren't in the fields, I have them doing the household work: washing clothes, cooking, cleaning, making repairs, everything. After all, they are from the Kol caste; that's what they do, work for Vasyas [people of a higher caste] like me. I give them food and a little land to work. They've also borrowed money, so I have to make sure that they stay on my land till it is paid back. ... I don't care how old they get—you can't just give money away! ...

There is nothing wrong in keeping bonded labor. They benefit from the system and so do I; even if agriculture is completely mechanized, I'll still keep my bonded laborers. You see, the way we do it I am like a father to these workers. It is a father-son relationship; I protect them and guide them. Sometimes I have to discipline them as well, just as a father would.[19]

are trafficked every year, mostly as agricultural workers, domestic workers, and prostitutes.[20] In a global perspective, the practice is concentrated in South and Southeast Asia, northern and western Africa, and parts of South America.[21] In raw numbers, the greatest national offenders are believed to be India, Pakistan, China, Mauritania, and Nepal.[22] Not surprisingly, there is a correlation between the presence of slavery within a country and such factors as poverty, political and legal corruption, and world views that permit some people to be seen as less valuable than others.

One helpful way to evaluate how well different nations are doing in resisting slavery is provided by the U.S. State Department's Office to Monitor and Combat Trafficking in Persons, which has set up a three-tier system in which it places each country based upon compliance with the United States's own Trafficking Victims Protection Act of 2000. There is also a fourth category—the Tier 2 Special Watch List—made up of countries who are doing a worse job than Tier 2 countries, but perhaps a better job than Tier 3 countries. Specifically, here are the qualifications for tier placement:

- *Tier 1:* Countries whose governments fully comply with the act's minimum standards.
- *Tier 2:* Countries whose governments do not fully comply with the act's minimum standards, but are making a significant effort to comply.
- *Tier 2 Special Watch List:* Countries whose governments do not fully comply with the act's minimum standards, but are making significant efforts to comply and for whom the absolute number of victims of severe forms of trafficking is significant or is significantly increasing, for whom there is no demonstrated evidence of increasing efforts to combat severe forms of trafficking in persons from the previous year, or for whom the determination that a country is making significant efforts to comply with the minimum standards was based on the country's commitments to take additional steps over the next year.
- *Tier 3:* Countries whose governments do not fully comply with the act's minimum standards and who are not making any efforts to comply.[23]

With its three-tier system, the State Department hopes to put pressure on nations around the world to improve their laws and law enforcement so that they might cease ranking so high as source, transit, or destination countries for human trafficking and as sites for internal trafficking. Nations placed on the Tier 2 Special Watch list know that they are under heightened scrutiny by the U.S. State Department. Those in Tier 3 risk losing aid money from the United States as well as from some international organizations, such as the World Bank, if they don't figure out how to earn a higher tier ranking. And this approach seems to be having some effect, as suggested by announcements by our government that the U.S. was moving a number of nations up from Tier 3 to the Tier 2 Special Watch List in recognition of their rapid response to State Department criticism.[24]

How Well Are the Nations Doing at Ending Slavery?

The following ranking reflects the placement of nations by the U.S. Office to Monitor and Combat Trafficking in Persons into its three-tier system, with Tier 1 being best and Tier 3 being worst. [25]

Tier 1

Australia	Hong Kong	Norway
Austria	Ireland	Poland
Belgium	Italy	Singapore
Canada	Lithuania	South Korea
Columbia	Luxembourg	Spain
Denmark	Malawi	Sweden
Finland	Morocco	Switzerland
France	The Netherlands	United Kingdom
Germany	New Zealand	

Tier 2

Afghanistan	Bulgaria	Costa Rica
Albania	Burkina Faso	Cote d'Ivoire
Angola	Burundi	Croatia
Azerbaijan	Cameroon	Czech Republic
Bangladesh	Chad	Dominican Republic
Belarus	Chile	East Timor
Benin	Congo (Democratic Repub-	Ecuador
Bosnia/Herzegovina	lic of Congo)	El Salvador
		Estonia

Tier 2 (cont'd)

Ethiopia	Macedonia	Rwanda
Gabon	Madagascar	Senegal
The Gambia	Mali	Serbia-Montenegro
Georgia	Malta	Sierra Leone
Ghana	Mauritius	Slovak Republic
Greece	Moldova	Slovenia
Guatemala	Mongolia	Sri Lanka
Guinea	Mozambique	Suriname
Guinea-Bissau	Nepal	Tajikistan
Guyana	Nicaragua	Tanzania
Honduras	Niger	Thailand
Hungary	Nigeria	Tunisia
Japan	Pakistan	Turkey
Jordan	Panama	Uganda
Kazakhstan	Paraguay	Ukraine
Kyrgyz Republic	Philippines	Uruguay
Latvia	Portugal	Vietnam
Lebanon	Romania	Yemen
		Zambia

Tier 2 Special Watch List

Algeria	Cyprus	Macau
Argentina	Egypt	Mexico
Armenia	Equatorial Guinea	Oman
Bahrain	India	Peru
Bolivia	Indonesia	Qatar
Brazil	Israel	Russia
Cambodia	Jamaica	South Africa
Central African Republic	Kenya	Taiwan
China (People's Republic of China)	Kuwait	Togo
	Libya	United Arab Emirates
Djibouti	Malaysia Mauritania	

	Tier 3	
Belize	*Laos*	*Syria*
Burma	*North Korea*	*Uzbekistan*
Cuba	*Saudi Arabia*	*Venezuela*
Iran	*Sudan*	*Zimbabwe*

The Business of Slavery

Isolated areas of improvement notwithstanding, human trafficking remains big business. The FBI estimates that trafficking generates $9.5 billion annually for organized crime syndicates around the world.[26] This makes it the third most profitable business for organized crime after illegal drugs and arms trafficking.[27] But most traffickers are less organized than they are criminal—they are engaged in what I call "disorganized organized crime." That is, they may operate as individuals, families, or small groups to take advantage of the localized economic opportunities that come with the combination of vulnerable persons and ready buyers. The total income from trafficking, then, must well exceed the FBI's estimate of $9.5 billion annually. One researcher has tentatively suggested that it might be $13 billion.[28]

Compared to the gross revenues of the world's largest industries, $13 billion is pocket change. For many people around the world, especially in poorer nations, the prospect of getting their hands on even a tiny fraction of the amount is more than enough to tempt them to get into trafficking or at least turn a blind eye to its occurrence. And so the wicked business goes on. The informational Web site www.HumanTrafficking.com calls trafficking "the fastest growing criminal industry in the world" and gives two primary reasons: (1) "high profits can be made quickly, with little or no start-up capital, and profits can be derived over a long period of time from the same victims (unlike drugs, which are quickly used up)"; and (2) "despite its criminal nature, the risk of prosecution is usually negligible."[29]

The conditions allowing slavery to exist, enriching some at the expense of others, are of both push and pull varieties. The pull, or market demand, side is easier to understand—and easier to despise. Greedy landowners and factory owners, for example, want cheap labor to increase their profit. Brothel customers and sex tourists like fresh girls. On the push side are all those conditions that make people vulnerable to enslavement. Of these, the greatest is undoubtedly poverty. Poverty gives parents the idea to do what otherwise ought to seem unimaginable—sell their children. Poverty leads to a lack of employment opportunities, which in turn suggests to rural young people that they ought to accept the big-city job offer that sounds too good to be true—and is. In addition to poverty, other factors may put people in a position of vulnerability to enslavement. Wars, political instability, and natural disasters can result in migration, which has been shown to increase trafficking. The obsolescence of traditional trades can make unskilled workers desperate to take any kind of work that is offered. Cultural patterns of discrimination against women and children can make them easy targets for exploitation by unscrupulous traffickers and those who are willing to make a quick buck (or peso or rupee).

With dynamics like these at play, there are many means by which people can find themselves enslaved. Sometimes they are abducted by strangers. For example, there have been cases of people who accepted a drugged drink from a new acquaintance and, after the drug had worn off, found themselves at a transit point on their way to the form of slavery someone else had picked out for them. More often, however, various tricks and ruses are employed. A young father may borrow money from a landlord and then be told that his family has to work for the landlord, to pay it off—and it will be "paid off" at the whim of the landlord if ever. Or a girl may be told by her parents that she is going to go on a visit to the big city with an "auntie," only to find that she has been sold by her parents and is expected to serve as a captive housekeeper in a rich family's home. Or a poor person may follow up the promise of a good job through an employment agency, and when he arrives at the factory, he finds that he cannot leave. Or a young woman may fall in love with a good-looking, smooth-tongued young man and agree to a fake marriage that quickly leads to her being sold by her "husband" and trafficked into a brothel.

Sometimes slaves escape or manage to buy themselves out of their bondage. Most of the time, though, their outcome is not so good. Emotionally or physically beaten down, they may reach a point where they can no longer resist their captivity. And, in the same perverse way that hostages can sometimes bond with their kidnappers, or that child abuse victims can emotionally attach to their abusers, slaves sometimes reach a point where they wouldn't change their status even if they could. Someone in debt bondage, for example, might not want to be responsible for earning his own living, since there is security of a sort in his bondage. Or a prostitute who was inducted into a brothel at a young age might eventually "graduate" to become a madam or a procurer of other young girls. The way that slaves themselves, not knowing any better, sometimes perpetuate the institution that enslaves them is one of the saddest results of their victimization.

Forms of Modern Slavery

The world's numerous cultures, religions, and world views guarantee that slavery will look different in diverse places around the globe—but not as different as you might expect. Indeed, the universal criminalization of slavery, along with the globalization of the economy, have enforced a certain sameness in the practices of slavery around the world. It is possible to identify several types of slavery that are essentially the same everywhere, though they may wear a different face in Cambodia versus Bolivia versus Pakistan.

Chattel slavery. This is the old-fashioned type of slavery, in which the slaveholder asserts ownership over the slave, who is kept in permanent servitude. In certain out-of-the-way places, such as rural areas of Mauritania, people are still held as chattel. By and large, though, this form of slavery is little known in our day.

Debt bondage. This form of slavery is as ancient as chattel slavery, but it has survived better and in fact is the most common type known today. It is the kind I encountered when I visited the Indian village at midnight and interviewed slaves on a pastor's rooftop. In debt bondage, a person pledges himself (or in the case of a parent needing money, pledges a child) against a loan of money, or even inherits the debt from a generation or more back, but the length and nature of the service are not defined and the labor does not actually reduce the original debt. The slave is perpetually paying back his debt and is never released from servitude—or at least not for a long time, when perhaps the slaveholder decides he does not want the slave anymore.

Contract slavery. This form is sneakier, offering a veneer of legality as employment so as to help the traffickers avoid prosecution. In contract slavery, a business owner offers a poor person a written contract for labor. Once the victim takes the "job," he finds that such is the power of control exerted by the boss that he can't get out of the work even if he wants to. If anyone comes by to question the employment, however, the "employer" can pull out the contract as proof that all is legal.

Sexual slavery and forced prostitution. Thanh-Dam Truong said that human trafficking reflects "an ongoing cultural decomposition of the human being, through a gradual removal of its spirit, personhood, vitality down to bare body parts."[30] This is more true in sex trafficking than in any other sort. Sexual slavery is a sort of extended form of rape in which one person maintains control of another and sexually abuses her. Forced prostitution occurs when someone is coerced or tricked into providing sexual services to others for pay that enriches the slaveholder. Sexual slavery is relatively rare, whereas forced prostitution is perhaps the second most common form of slavery today, after debt bondage.

In addition to these more common forms of slavery, there are also others practiced in different parts of the world. These include *war slavery* (people are taken against their will to join an army), *domestic slavery* (a woman may be sold to take care of someone else's home), and *religious slavery* (someone is dedicated to serving a religious institution or acting as a religious prostitute, as in the case of the devadasis we will look at more closely in chapter four).

These categories do not necessarily comprise a comprehensive list. Nor are they mutually exclusive—for example, a bogus contract might be used to mask debt bondage, or a domestic slave might be subjected to sexual abuse by her captor. Moreover, slavery is gradually evolving in response to changing economic realities. As investigators look into alleged cases of slavery around the world, they find that the victimization usually can be assigned to one of these categories.

The Youngest Victims

What particularly breaks my heart is the way in which children are swept into each of the contemporary kinds of slavery. In many areas, children are actually preferred as slaves, for example to crawl into narrow mine openings, to operate machinery that has small parts, and to satisfy the lust of pedophiles. I'm certainly not saying that it's all right for an adult to be made a slave, but the heartlessness of the trafficker seems all the worse when his victim is a child—and the costs borne by the victim are likely to be much greater as liberty, innocence, and health are taken away before the child barely has a chance to begin living.

According to the International Labor Organization, 8.4 million children are involved in what it labels the "unconditional worst forms of child labour." Breaking it down further, the ILO found the following numbers of children engaged in terrible labor activities:

- forced and bonded labor—5.7 million
- prostitution and pornography—1.8 million
- illicit activities (such as drug trafficking)—0.6 million
- armed conflict—0.3 million

The ILO also estimates that each year 1.2 million children are trafficked, that is, transported so that their labor may be appropriated by others for some purpose.[31]

UNICEF, in its report titled *Excluded and Invisible*, comments, "Trafficking of children takes many different forms. Some children are forcibly abducted, others are tricked and still others opt to let themselves be trafficked, seduced by the promise of earnings but not suspecting the level of exploitation they will suffer at the other end of the recruiting chain. Trafficking always involves a journey, whether within a country—from the rural areas to a tourist resort, for example—or across an international border. At the final destination, trafficked children become part of an underground world of illegality into which they effectively disappear."[32]

That's what slavery is like for all its victims—a kind of pit into which lives are cast, sometimes never to be seen again. We can only imagine what these people might have become if they had been allowed to flourish in freedom.

Slavery's Effects on Slaves—and the Rest of Us

Slavery is a human rights violation of the worst and most basic sort. Beyond being wrong, it is also harmful in a myriad of ways. Mainly, of course, it is the slaves themselves who bear the brunt of the suffering caused by their servitude. However, we are all connected in this world, and the harm done to slaves radiates outward to affect the rest of us in some way. When we consider the necessity for ending slavery in its modern-day forms, then, these are the reasons why.[34]

Psychological damage. The damage suffered in a slave's mind and spirit because of his fettered state is not easy to observe or measure, but it is by no means the least kind of harm he may sustain. The type of slavery to which he is subjected, and the length of time he must endure it, help to determine how severe his psychological damage might become as well as the forms it might take. Counselors who have provided aftercare to rescued slave victims report such problems as depression, suicidal intentions, low self-esteem, hopelessness, anger, delinquency, and an inability to make decisions.

**Victim Profile:
Mary,
a Child Soldier**

Mary, a sixteen-year-old demobilized soldier forced to join an armed rebel group in central Africa, remembers: "I feel so bad about the things that I did. It disturbs me so much that I inflicted death on other people. When I go home I must do some traditional rites because I have killed. I must perform these rites and cleanse myself. I still dream about the boy from my village whom I killed. I see him in my dreams, and he is talking to me, saying I killed him for nothing, and I am crying." [33]

Physical harm. It is no wonder that the life of a slave is often a short one. Being forced to live in crowded, unsanitary conditions, often with little or no medical care, is an invitation to disease. Many slaves put to work in such places as mines, factories, and quarries are subject to unsafe working conditions and suffer injuries at an alarming rate. Children who are given inadequate nutrition experience stunted growth, as in the case of camel jockeys in the Middle East who are deliberately starved to keep them small. Slaves put to work as beggars may be purposely maimed so as to increase the generosity of passersby. Prostitutes frequently suffer gynecological damage and are exposed to sexually transmitted diseases, including HIV/AIDS.

Social breakdown. Enslavement cuts so deeply into families and communities that the wounds can take generations to heal if ever. When a desire for financial gain causes parents to sell their children, trust has been lost, a family unit has been divided, and friends have been separated. Moreover, once a tradition of trafficking has become established in a certain village or other locale, it typically is perpetuated, diminishing the community permanently.

Criminal expansion. Modern-day slavery fuels organized crime on both a large and a small scale. Trafficking may be connected to other illegal activities, such as document forgery, money laundering, and drug sales. The law enforcement officers who ought to oppose the criminal activities often become involved in them through taking bribes or even by directly participating in the trafficking. The government's attempts to exercise authority are thus undermined, and as a result, people find themselves living in an environment filled with corruption and lawlessness.

Economic costs. Slaves typically are poorly educated people who work at low-skilled jobs that enrich nobody but their slaveholders. Their productivity is low because they have little opportunity to improve themselves and little incentive to compete in the workforce. When they need medical care and other services, it usually is the society that pays. Thus, the slaves remain mired in poverty and are a drag on their nation's economy, instead of becoming the productive workers, liberal consumers, and faithful taxpayers that they might otherwise have been.

One day, in Southern India, I had the opportunity to investigate a large stone quarry in Tamil Nadu. Because I had a video camera with me, the mudalali must have assumed that I was a journalist with an international magazine and invited me to come in and film the corps of slaves he had working for him. With camera rolling, I walked into a huge pit, which could not be seen from the road, and filmed whole families—men, women, and children—crushing larger rocks into smaller rocks in the sweltering heat. These rocks would then be hauled in baskets to nearby trucks for delivery. The mudalali told me that the rate he was paying was less than fifty cents for each backbreaking day.

This is what slavery reduces human beings to. This is why it cannot be permitted to survive.

Abolition Now

Many people are hardly aware that slavery and slavery-like conditions exist in our day, or if they are aware, the problem seems so remote to them that they are unmotivated to do anything about it. Numerous national and international organizations exist in part or in whole to oppose

Victim Profile: Neary, a Forced Prostitute

Neary grew up in rural Cambodia. Her parents died when she was a child, and in an effort to give her a better life, her sister married her off when she was seventeen. Three months later they went to visit a fishing village. Her husband rented a room in what Neary thought was a guesthouse. But when she woke the next morning, her husband was gone. The owner of the house told her she had been sold by her husband for three hundred dollars and that she was actually in a brothel.

For five years, Neary was raped by five to seven men every day. In addition to brutal physical abuse, Neary was infected with HIV and contracted AIDS. The brothel threw her out when she became sick, and she eventually found her way to a local shelter. She died of HIV/AIDS at the age of twenty-three.[35]

forced labor, but they are often so bureaucratic and so influenced by politics that they don't seem to be able to do much about the problem either. Nongovernmental organizations are nimbler, but I have found that many of them are focused upon performing research and disseminating information about the slavery problem. That's great as far as it goes. I'm all for raising awareness of slavery—that's what this book is for, after all—but at some point early on, we need to get to the *do* part.

That's what my colleagues and I are about. We want to do more than just talk about the problem. We don't want to merely set up offices, buy computers, and order business cards. We're not interested in mission statements and endless group think. We want to do.

If you are reading this book, perhaps you are already involved in, or about to get to, the *do* part. My encouragement to you? Do it!

We can't just be patient and wait and hope for change; we have to do something if slavery is to be ended, or at least severely curtailed, in our lifetimes. Just as abolitionists in the nineteenth century banded together to outlaw slavery, so today like-minded people need to come together and find ways to end slave practices that are taking place outside the law. Indeed, as we now know, passing an act of Congress or Parliament was insufficient to end the practice of slavery; it only criminalized it and drove it underground. The abolition movement of the nineteenth century, then, merely started the process of ending slavery. We must complete what others began by ending slavery in fact as well as in law. We need to raise the stakes for the bad guys and take the fight to them. It's high time that humanity rids the planet of this blot once and for all.

Some get it. One young British writer, speaking from the Christian tradition, stated, "A globalised world means that we have to respond to 'do unto others as you would have done unto yourself' on a wider horizon than maybe fifty years ago. If you were waiting on your pimp to count the condoms after a day's work to ensure that you had worked hard enough, the consequences of which were being beaten to within an inch of your life, what would you want someone to do for you? If you had been sold as a bonded laborer and were forced to roll two thousand *beedi* cigarettes for a dime each day under threat of physical injury, what would you want to have happen? Should they buy a computer first? Design business cards and a web page before springing to action? Releasing the captives and liberating the oppressed might not be as metaphorical as we once understood."[36] It's about *doing* unto others, not just thinking about it or feeling compassion or discussing the topic.

My response to the problem of slavery, after encountering it in India several years ago, has been to form Restore International and, after finding and picking the best of the best, putting those brave and talented people to work in the field. I tell the story of Restore and how it works in part two of this book. Before we get there, however, I want to expose in more detail one of the particular types of slavery upon which we have chosen to focus. In official discussions of this kind of victimization, it often goes by the bland acronym CSEC, standing for the "commercial sexual exploitation of children." In plainer terms, it is the rape of kids. This is the kind of crime committed against Karishma, and it is horrendous.

Not only have we been focused upon this one type of slavery—forced child prostitution—but we have also been focused upon debt bondage and the absence of access to justice for kids and the poorest of the poor. Restore International is currently active in two countries. The first is the largest slaveholding country in the world: India. The second is a country torn by civil war for more than two decades: Uganda.

There are thousands upon thousands of Karishmas in India. There are little girls bearing different names in countless other countries. They are victims of caste stigma, chauvinistic bias, tribalism, and economic deprivation on a huge scale. Understanding their plight reveals the worst of human behavior—and helps us understand the importance of offering hope for restoration to liberty and to life.

THREE

Rape for Profit

Child Prostitution in India

My daughter, Lindsey, wrote the following in 2003, when she was fifteen years old.

> The weariness settled over me, weighing me down physically and emotionally. We had been awake and traveling from Chennai since six o'clock that morning, a long sixteen hours ago. Now here we were, in a small rented van, as we began the two-hour drive into the red-light area of the city of Mumbai, India.
>
> Outside the car window, the street was packed with bright-yellow rickshaws, motorcycles, and a crush of people moving by. Men ambled along, crowding into each other, and women holding babies wrapped in rags knocked on car windows, begging for food or money.
>
> The thick air, smelling of sweat, curry, exhaust, and dust, seeped in through the closed window. I sat pressed between my dad and our friends, feeling pensive about where we were going tonight. Being scared never entered my mind, though, because not only was I with my dad and brother, but also we had with us our friends and I knew they wouldn't let any harm come to us.
>
> "There's a brothel up there," our friend said, pointing to one of the dark buildings next to us. "We raided this one last December, but unfortunately someone tipped them off.

"A lot of times you will see a group of girls gathered around a storefront, and there will be a dark staircase next to them that leads up to the brothel," he explained as we passed a few more buildings.

"Those girls over there—are they prostitutes?" I asked.

About twenty girls were crowded around a dark stairwell next to the entrance to a store called Sharp Electric. I felt an immediate ache inside, realizing that those girls were my age.

Then the horror of it hit me: in this city of Mumbai, on the other side of the world from my home in the United States, almost every girl outside my window was a prostitute and almost every man was either a pimp or a customer. I felt choked with tears and then numb. This was beyond anything I had ever seen.

Some of the brothels were arranged like stalls, with rooms open to the street and a sheet hanging over the entryway. I spotted a girl only a few yards away, standing in front of a dimly lit green room. She appeared to be no older than me and was wearing a dark-blue sari draped over her thin shoulders. If you traded the sari for jeans and a T-shirt, the grimy building for the fresh white ones of my school back home, the shadows of Mumbai for the San Diego sunshine, this girl could have been one of my friends.

The young girl spotted the video camera as we drove past and covered her face, turning to run inside the brothel. As she disappeared behind the curtain, I pictured her as one of my friends. If roles had been reversed, she could have been one of the girls I went to school with.

I realized that these thousands of young girls in India were my peers, friends, and sisters, trapped on the other side of the world.

I include these observations from Lindsey, not only because I am proud of my daughter's perceptiveness, but also because they preserve the first impressions made on her by India's child prostitution problem. Those who, like me, have worked with the problem for a while can become used to this terrible scourge, even if we never grow comfortable with it. And you, reading this book, with its facts and statistics, might tend to view the problem in an objective fashion. Its almost like our own internal defense mechanism takes over and wants to let us see these precious lives in some other fashion, because we cannot fathom the horror and the reality of what these individuals endure every day. The truth (and this is what Lindsey's reflections present so well) is that child prostitution is a *terrible* thing that is *really* happening *every day* to girls just like my daughter. And it will continue happening until we do something to stop it.

Every form of modern-day slavery, wherever it occurs in the world, is an outrage, an assault upon God-given human dignity. If one form of slavery is more obviously evil than others, it must be the sexual exploitation of kids—kids around the age of my daughter, kids like Karishma. Our work in India with bonded laborers and our work in other countries where those in power take advantage of the weak has been compelling to me personally, as well as challenging. Perhaps it is because I am a dad, or perhaps it is because I am a human, but of the abuses I have been exposed to thus far, to me the most representative example of the gross abuse of God's handiwork in people is the forcing of girls to sell their bodies against their will. I propose, therefore, to use child prostitution in India as a sort of case study to explore how a form of modern-day slavery can develop in a given area, what effects it can have on individuals and the society, and what responses to it are most helpful.

The Youngest Members of the Oldest Profession

India's reputation as a land teeming with people is well earned. According to the most recent census carried out by the Indian government, the population of the nation in 2001 was just over 1 billion people.[1] Due to its higher rate of birth, India is expected to surpass China as the most populous nation on earth by the year 2050, when India will have a population of more than 1.5 billion people. Considering a population so large, it comes as no surprise that the number of people involved with prostitution in India is large as well.

Understandably, reliable statistics on the sex trade in India are hard to come by. The U.S. State Department estimates that more than 2.3 million girls and women work as prostitutes in India. Of these, about 500,000—or around 22 percent of all Indian prostitutes—are under the age of eighteen. India thus accounts for half of the estimated 1 million children engaged in the sex trade worldwide.[2] And, since many of India's adult prostitutes have aged into their majority while working as prostitutes, this means that far more than 22 percent of the Indian females who are currently engaged in prostitution were under the age of eighteen at the time of their initial exploitation.

India is the hub for sex trafficking in its region and is a source, transit, and destination country. Indian women and children are trafficked to such areas as the Gulf States, Australia, Malaysia, Singapore, Europe, and the United States. In Mumbai, children as young as nine are bought at auctions where Arabs bid against Indian men.[3] Because of India's relatively open borders, major trafficking routes have been established between the nation and its neighbors Bangladesh, Nepal, Pakistan, and Sri Lanka.[4] According to a 2003 United Nations report, India is one of the top nine destination countries for sex trafficking in the world.[5] One major survey of prostitutes working in the brothels of India showed that 10 percent of them had been brought in from other nations, with around 2 percent of them being Bangladeshi and 2.5 percent being Nepalese.[6]

A thirteen-year-old girl from Nepal was offered a job as a domestic worker in India, but when she arrived in Mumbai, she was taken to a brothel on Mumbai's infamous Falkland Road. At first refusing to have sex with customers, she was locked in a small, windowless room without food or water. After the girl spent four days in isolation, one of the madam's *goondas* (thugs) came in and banged her head against the concrete floor until she lost consciousness. Later she was raped by the *goonda* until she complied with her captors' demands to service their customers.[7]

The great majority of child sex victims are girls, but boys are not immune. For example, young boys who have been abandoned or sold by their parents may fall into the hands of a society of eunuchs, or *hijras*, who take them into the jungle and cut off their genitals in a ceremony ironically called *nirvana*. Thousands of eunuchs are prostituting themselves in India's major cities. They are often more willing to perform high-risk sex acts than are female prostitutes, and some men mistakenly believe they cannot contract HIV from eunuchs.[8]

India has also become a major destination for sex tourism. One report stated, "In southern India, two popular destinations emerging for pedophile activity are Kovalam in Kerala and Mammallpuram in Tamil Nadu. Goa is a popular destination for pedophiles looking for sex with boys. There has been a reported increase in sex tourism from the Gulf States to India in the past three decades. Young men from the Gulf States have come to India for sexual relations with Indian women. New Zealand men in India have been charged with child sexual abuse."[9]

One twelve-year-old victim of sex tourism explained her situation to a social worker. "I am accompanying JF [a German tourist] for the last five years. He says that he will marry me. He gives money to my family.

My family is in Hyderabad. He has sex with me regularly. Initially it was painful and I used to cry. Now it is a daily routine."[10]

Prostitution operates in many different venues. The prostitutes might work out of rooms, apartments, small hotels, exclusive clubs, massage parlors, and dance clubs. The majority, however, work out of brothels. Among Indian brothels, there are three categories, classified as A, B, and C.[11]

A-grade brothels are the "best" kind of brothels, employing as call girls both trafficking victims and voluntary prostitutes who do the work because the money is good. These brothels typically have the best facilities and employ the most attractive girls, and they also charge the highest rates, often sending the girls out to wealthy businessmen and tourists. The rate for an hour with one of the call girls from an A-grade brothel can range from 1,000 to 2,500 rupees (about $22.50 to $56.50).[12]

B-grade brothels exist in red-light districts and have comparatively good facilities, including such amenities as televisions and air conditioning. The prostitutes are often trafficking victims. The rate for an hour with a prostitute in one of these brothels usually runs from around 200 to 375 rupees (about $4.50 to $8.50).

And then there are the C-grade brothels, the worst of the lot. They are tiny, dirty, and unhygienic, often teeming with insects. Again, the prostitutes are mostly trafficked. The cost of an hour with a prostitute in one of these brothels is around 100 to 200 rupees (about $2.00 to $4.00). These are the kinds of places where Restore International most often performs its rescues, since these are the most common brothels and they contain the greatest number of underage girls. We found Karishma in a brothel like this.

The amounts for the individual brothel transactions can seem ridiculously low to a Westerner, but they add up. A 1999 report estimated that the total transactions in prostitution at that time were 185 million rupees ($4.18 million) per day.[13] More than a quarter of that amount is believed to be earned through the commercial sexual exploitation of children.[14] Minor prostitutes are more highly valued by customers and therefore bring in more money for their captors than do most adult prostitutes.

Some of the bad characters whom we have had to deal with, and who advocate on behalf of the perpetrators, will argue that prostitution is a business like any other and that, even when it comes to minors participating in the business, it's not so bad. However, in India, sex with an underage person is legally defined as rape, and by any reasonable moral measure, the forced prostitution of children is an abomination.[15] We can easily

Victim Profile: Yauvani

Yauvani is from the village of Kapilagodi in South India and is an only child.[16] Her father's name is Samendra and her mother's name is Sanjana. Her parents own a grocery shop in their village. Yauvani is a quiet girl, seventeen or eighteen years old, and is a devadasi (religious prostitute). When she was living at home, she did not attend school but rather earned money by making *gajras* (flower garlands).

When Yauvani was twelve, a relative told her about the profession of prostitution. She and her friend Disha, who has since died of a fever, traveled by bus to Sangli in order to engage in the profession. At the time, her parents were not aware of the decision Yauvani had made.

Yauvani lived in the same brothel as another girl, Madhura. They both did their own cooking and cleaning. Yauvani was paid 50 rupees (about $1.13) per customer and had two or three customers a day. She paid 300 rupees (about $6.75) for rent each month and sent 200 to 300 rupees home every month. *Along with Madhura, Yauvani was rescued from the brothel when it was raided by the police and Restore International.*

(cont'd on next page)

understand how extreme poverty, combined with other vulnerabilities, might tempt some people to exploit others or to allow themselves to be exploited. But, that never makes it right. It has been said that the oldest profession is the oldest oppression, and that is certainly true for the kids who are tricked, coerced, or persuaded into that kind of work.

The Exploiters Exposed

Researcher Alison Phinney summarized, "Sex trafficking is driven by a demand for women's and children's bodies in the sex industry, fueled by a supply of women who are denied equal rights and opportunities for education and economic advancement and perpetuated by traffickers who are able to exploit human misfortune with near impunity."[17] When it comes to sex trafficking, there is plenty of blame to go around.

The trafficking hierarchy. As in other organized crime operations, trafficking is hierarchical. In the larger trafficking organizations, there are at least four levels:

- kingpins
- primary traffickers
- secondary traffickers
- "spotters"

In addition to these major players in the trafficking business, others provide support services to the organization. These include the following:

- money men who finance transactions
- *goondas* who provide security
- hoteliers who provide accommodations during transit
- transporters who arrange transportation

- medical personnel (sometimes quacks)
- who attend to the needs of victims during transit
- public officials who let traffickers through immigration and security

All of these play important roles, but it is the traffickers in the four chief levels who really make it all happen.[18]

The kingpin corresponds to the mafia don in Western organized crime. He sets up the trafficking network, appoints primary traffickers, and manages all of the organization's activities. For this, he extracts the highest level of profit from the trade. His risks are great if he were ever to be caught, but he protects himself with personal security as well as connections to politicians and law enforcement officers who can insulate him from prosecution. To the public, he remains largely anonymous. In the 1990s, however, reporter Robert I. Friedman managed to blow away some of the haze surrounding such kingpins when he investigated the criminal workings behind the massive red-light operations centered on Falkland Road in Mumbai.

Friedman learned that Mumbai's flesh trade was controlled by four separate crime groups—one that paid off the police, a second that controlled moneylending, a third that maintained order in the red-light district, and a fourth that procured women and girls from throughout India and neighboring countries. The four crime groups all cooperated because everybody was getting rich, and the kingpins didn't mind sharing some of the wealth with police officers and politicians in order to keep the rupees rolling in. Proof of official collusion was on display when one of the four kingpins, Mehboob Thasildar, the procurer of women, held a gala to celebrate the

Although Yauvani had entered the brothel voluntarily, she had come to see what a hard life it was and wanted out. Furthermore, Yauvani was pregnant by a married customer. So, with her family's support, she has returned home to deliver her child. Yauvani desires to return to her job of making *gajras* and perhaps to work on farms.

opening of a restaurant in his block-long bordello. The event was attended by a Member of Parliament, the Minister of Housing for the state of Maharashtra, and two state assemblymen.

Friedman met with Brij Mohan Sharma, the mob boss who ran internal security in the red-light district. On that occasion, Friedman told Sharma of his estimate that the red-light district generated $400 million dollars per year in revenue. (The reporter had arrived at that estimate by calculating 100,000 girls working 365 days per year, averaging six customers a day, at $2 a trick.) Sharma replied, "It's more than that!" and added that the profits were plowed into gold and real estate.[19]

The first level of workers under such kingpins as these are the primary traffickers. They are the workers who manage the individual transactions, taking orders from brothel owners, deploying lesser traffickers, making purchases, scheduling transportation, and selling the "goods" to pimps or brothel owners. In short, they are the merchants of the flesh trade.

The primary traffickers work closely with secondary traffickers and "spotters." These petty criminals operate at the grassroots level, gathering information and acquiring girls. The spotters visit markets, villages, railway stations, bus stations, and other places where they can find vulnerable people for trafficking. The secondary traffickers then arrange to buy or lure the girls into the trafficking racket.

Often the traffickers are looking for a specific kind of girl to fulfill a request made by a brothel keeper. Some of the factors that purchasers might include in their request are the following: physical appearance (good looks), age (younger girls and virgins are more in demand), region (girls from a particular area of India are preferred in certain brothels), complexion (fair-skinned girls are preferred), and submissiveness.[20] It is the secondary traffickers who are out in the field trying to fill the orders they have received, and so it is these people who are most likely to come into direct contact with the girls.

The field traffickers are about evenly divided between young men and middle-aged women, and most of them have been involved in the sex trade for years as brothel owners or pimps, or else they have inherited the business from older relatives. For them, making money is the motive and exercising power over the weak adds spice. These people have been so warped by the work they do that, in a survey, a large number of them openly admitted to having trafficked their own relatives—their wives, sisters, daughters, nieces, or cousins—for money.[21]

One trafficker expressed the cold mercenary motivation for what he does: "I bring new children to my customers every day. I get 2,000 to 3,500 rupees per child. I am operating on the basis of the market demand. It does not bother me, whether it is a child. If I get equal money to sell something else, I will do that as well."[22]

The traffickers know their business. They operate year-round, but take special advantage of difficult periods, such as before a harvest or during a drought, when people are looking for extra income to survive. They go to places where they are more likely to find vulnerable girls, including areas where there is widespread poverty and unemployment, where there is a tradition of trafficking, or where law enforcement is lax. Then they look for individual girls who appear ripe for the picking, such as those who live in deprived circumstances or who come from broken homes. The trafficker approaches a targeted girl and adapts his strategy to what he knows of her. More than half the time traffickers will lure their victims by offering jobs or money. Other common techniques include making false promises of marriage, pretending to become friends with girls, and if all else fails, kidnapping the victims.[23]

The large number of missing children reported to police in India, some of whom are eventually found in brothels, testifies to the fact that some children are simply abducted.[24] Since in most cases the trafficker uses persuasion or trickery, before they leave town with the girls, they make the deal "official." That is, they hand over a payment of money to the parents or other family members of the new brothel slave. The sum is usually equal to less than 10 percent of what the trafficker earns. "Such is the vulnerability of the victim and her parents that she can be 'purchased' for paltry sums."[25]

After the purchase of a victim has been completed, the girl is usually transported to another city or state or even across national borders. This often means temporarily stopping over at a transit site, such as a home or hotel room, perhaps for days or even for weeks. Sadly, at this point the "breaking in" process usually starts—and the girl at last realizes what she has gotten into. The previously friendly trafficker may turn much more brutal. Males in the trafficking network will begin raping the girl (unless they want to preserve her virginity in order to get a higher price for her). She may also be forced to watch pornography and be instructed in how to please customers. And if she resists, she may be tortured.

One researcher reported numerous forms of violence used against females trafficked for prostitution. They may be bound, beaten, starved, locked in a dark room, burnt with cigarettes, strangled, or stabbed. Sometimes attempts are made to create a dependency on drugs and alcohol. They may also be threatened with torture and physical abuse against themselves or their families, and they may in fact be murdered if they do not cooperate.[26] Another researcher commented, "Children relent within seven to ten days under psychological pressure."[27]

A prostitute named Shanta remembered what she observed of a nine-year-old Nepalese girl's initiation into prostitution. "She was a scared little thing. Really tiny. She was thrashed till her nose bled. Then a man was sent into the room she was locked up in. Her screams had us shivering. She was torn apart, couldn't walk for weeks," recalled Shanta, her voice shaking at the recollection.[28]

When a girl has been forced into submission, she can be transported the rest of the way to the brothel that is her destination. There the transaction is completed. The average price for a virgin is around 10,000 rupees (about $225) and around half of that for a non-virgin. Not that the girl herself will ever see any of this money. In fact, she is usually told by her new keeper that she will have to work until she can pay back the sum that was paid for her.

Red-light district exploiters. Once the trafficked girl arrives at the brothel, she falls into the hands of another set of exploiters. These include brothel keepers, pimps, johns, and corrupt police and local officials. Under their handling, the girl completes her initiation into her new life of captivity and degradation.

Brothels in India are usually small shacks or stalls called *dhabas*. The one who owns or rents the facility is not necessarily the one who manages the work that takes place there, though often she is. The one who manages the operations is usually called a *brothel keeper* or *brothel manager*.[29] Most brothel keepers are women in their thirties or forties, and two-thirds of them were formerly prostitutes themselves.[30] You might think that these women would understand the suffering of their charges better than anyone, but it seems that spending so long in this environment has affected their thinking to the point where they believe that the sex trade is natural and that the best they can do is to get themselves on the side of making more money out of it. The fact is, the brothel keepers are almost all uneducated, illiterate women who know no other life and cannot imagine making a living in any other business.

Brothel keepers make contact with traffickers to acquire new girls. They manage, on average, six or seven women and girls in their brothels. Most like to have, and do have, underage girls in their brothels, because these girls are the most profitable. They will sometimes send girls outside the brothels to places like hotels, guesthouses, and private homes in response to specific requests, since these off-sites rendezvous with wealthy Indians or tourists often pay more than those that take place in the brothels. They take the money from the customers, use some of it to pay off traffickers, use more of it to bribe police officers, spend some of it on food, cosmetics, clothing, and other supplies, and use the rest to give the girls a pittance (if anything) before keeping the rest for themselves.

Some brothel keepers try to win over their new girls with kindness. Many others, however, use scolding and abuse or beat up the girls with the help of *goondas*. They may also put them in solitary confinement or resort to torture to get the cooperation they want. The frequency with which beatings are reported proves that girls try to resist their abuse strenuously for a while, until they give up hope.

Closely allied with the brothel keepers are the pimps. These are men who operate in the red-light districts and steer customers to one or more brothels that are paying them a fee for doing so. They ask the customers what they are looking for, showcase the qualities of the prostitutes, and answer questions the customers have about the brothel or the transaction. Pimps often double as small-time traffickers.

Most brothel keepers bribe corrupt police officers, either by giving them small payments (called *haftas*) on a regular basis or by offering them free sex with the prostitutes. In turn, the police turn a blind eye to the illegal activity taking place. They will also give the brothel keepers advance notice on raids, so that the keepers can take the girls away or else hide them in attics, cubicles, storerooms, or other specially designed hideouts. We experienced such corruption firsthand when we attempted repeatedly to rescue Karishma, only to learn that the brothel owners, with whom the police had struck a bargain, were tipped off by the police of an impending raid to rescue this precious girl.

The customers at brothels are the ultimate source of demand fueling the sex trade, including the trafficking of kids for prostitution.[31] The customers are men, mostly in their twenties and thirties, from a wide range of social and economic backgrounds. They may be students, laborers, businessmen, truck drivers, or tourists, and most of them are frequent customers in the brothel areas. Reportedly, demand goes up at festival seasons, when people flock to the cities and larger towns, as well as after harvests, when farm workers have more money in their pockets.

Most customers arrive at brothels with a particular kind of prostitute in mind. The conductors of a survey with brothel clientele reported, "There

Victim Profile: Anahita

Anahita is eighteen or nineteen years old and comes from the Bagalkot district of Karnataka state.[35] She is the oldest of three daughters in her family. Her father, Mahaniya, is unemployed. He used to work as a driver, until he was blinded in an accident. Her mother, Madhuksara, is a housewife. Anahita is a devadasi and can speak the languages of Kannada, Hindi, and Marathi. When she lived in her village, she did housework to earn a living.

At the age of twelve or thirteen, with her parents' permission, Anahita and five of her friends went to Kolhapur on a visit. While they were roaming around in Kolhapur, they met a girl named Diksha. Unaware that she was a prostitute in Gokul Nagar, the red-light district of Sangli, Anahita and her friends accepted Diksha's invitation to stay with her in her home near the Kolhapur bus station while they were in town. During their stay with Diksha, Anahita shared with Diksha about her family situation in Bagalkot and gave Diksha her home address. Two days after Anahita and her friends returned home from their stay in Kolhapur, Diksha

(cont'd on next page)

is an all-pervasive assertion of male power and machismo. It is important to note that 53.3 per cent of the respondents stated that they looked forward to having sex with girls who are submissive and willing to surrender to all their demands. This included acquiescing to all their perversions, being ready to have sex without condoms and catering to their clients' pleasure needs. It is also significant that 38.8 per cent of the respondents preferred young girls because of their fear of HIV/AIDS and other such deadly diseases. Many of them were looking for cures [due to the prevalent myth that having sex with young girls cures AIDS], while others wanted to make sure that they would not contract the disease."[32]

Most clients pay between 100 and 500 rupees per visit with a prostitute, more if she is young and especially if she is a virgin.[33] Many of them also offer tips, called *bakshish*, or gifts such as cosmetics, jewelry, or liquor, either as a reward for submitting to demeaning acts or as a bribe to buy extra time with the girl. Although in the raids that we conducted with the police in the Gokul Nagar red-light district of Sangli a number of johns were arrested, on balance very few johns are arrested or even see a police presence in or around a red-light district.

With the johns, the prostitutes come up against their final exploiters, the ones who created the demand that put them into the hands of a trafficker back at the beginning of their exploitation.

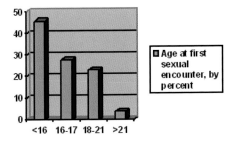

Figure 3.1: Trafficked victims age at first sexual encounter.[34]

Causes of Child Prostitution

The participants in the trafficking network could not operate as they do if it were not for an environment that makes it possible for the sex trafficking of minors to exist. Many factors in Indian society combine to account for the large number of girls who wind up being raped for profit.

Poverty, ignorance, and the caste system. Every nation has its rich and its poor, but in India the gap between the two seems more obvious and more extreme than almost anywhere else. Tens of millions of Indian families survive on annual incomes that wouldn't cover the monthly rent of an apartment in the United States. There have been reports of middle and upper-class teens in India voluntarily engaging in prostitution on occasion in order to raise extra spending money. And runaways and other minors from any socioeconomic level are vulnerable to being abducted into prostitution by organized crime rings. It is the children from poor families who most often show up in India's brothels.

The amount that can be earned by selling a girl into prostitution is not great by Western standards, but it is enough to be appealing to

arrived at Anahita's home. She told Anahita about a good-paying tailoring job and asked her to go with her and take this job. Anahita's parents agreed to let her go in order for her to help support the family.

Anahita went with Diksha to Gokul Nagar in Sangli. When Anahita asked Diksha about the promised tailoring job, Diksha admitted that she had lied. Diksha then informed her that the work available was in prostitution and that she had to remain there and be a prostitute. Undoubtedly, Diksha was receiving money for trafficking a new girl into the brothel system.

Believing that this was the only way to help feed her family, Anahita decided to stay at the brothel. She had about four customers a day, earning from 100 to 150 rupees (about $2.25 to $3.50) a day. The hope of supporting her family was not feasible, as she was unable to send money home, due to her low earnings as well as her monthly rent payment of 300 rupees ($6.75) and other expenses. Additionally, a brothel keeper would collect money from her and the other girls from time to time. Diksha died in Kolhapur two months after Anahita came to Gokul Nagar

(cont'd on next page)

Anahita was rescued from Gokul Nagar in a raid instigated by Restore International and is currently living in an aftercare facility. She says that she no longer wants to be involved with prostitution and is willing to be trained in other trades, such as stitching. Although she desires to return to her home, she is unsure about whether she will be happy living with her family again. She said, "If my parents had taken good care of me, would I have ended up in prostitution?"

poor families of India. Parents and other relatives often jump at the chance to receive the equivalent of several months' income in exchange for giving up a girl child who is otherwise likely to wind up costing them more money than she could bring in through another kind of employment. The girls themselves often feel they must submit to prostitution in order to raise money for themselves and their families, and so they may voluntarily go into the brothels. Frequently the money they are permitted by their "landlords" to keep is barely sufficient to cover their own living expenses, much less enable them to send anything home—but they don't know this at the outset.

A link between poverty and prostitution has been conclusively proved by the Asian Development Bank, which has stated, "An examination of the highest source for trafficking of women and children in Southern India reveals that trafficking is more common in areas that are prone to drought or other natural disasters, situated in less productive agro-climatic zones and where large numbers of families live below the poverty line. Those who make low wages, if any, are functionally landless; one third of women and girls in CSW [commercial sex work] in metropolitan cities were from drought prone-areas, clearly supporting the link between poverty, powerlessness, and vulnerability to trafficking."[36]

Furthermore, according to the Asian Development Bank, poverty in India is becoming feminized. In other words, in India, women are poorer than men, their poverty is more severe, and their poverty is increasing compared to men's.[37] The bank report further states, "It can … be argued that the feminization of poverty in South Asia is accompanied by the feminization of survival strategies. In hard times, women are more likely than men to exploit every possibility for work or income, including precarious activities and poorly paid work at home or in the informal sector (including provision of sexual services)."[38]

Poverty also contributes to sex trafficking indirectly in that it is connected to low levels of education. People who have less schooling and perhaps cannot read are more vulnerable to being taken in by traffickers' ruses and are less aware of the legal and other resources offered by the Indian government to trafficking victims. Lack of marketable skills may make uneducated girls think that the only work they are qualified for is prostitution—that all they've got to sell is their bodies. And in the cases of the customers of prostitution, a lack of education about HIV/AIDS transmission has tragically led to the superstition that sexual relations with virgins or young children will cure the illness.

There is also a close connection between poverty and India's caste system. While India's Constitution forbids public discrimination on the basis of caste,[39] social ranking remains a deeply embedded feature of Indian culture and daily life.[40] The 16 percent of the population that belong to the Dalit groups (the so-called "untouchables") often live in extreme poverty. So it comes as no surprise that a major report on Indian women and girls in prostitution showed that nearly 50 percent were from scheduled castes and scheduled tribes and from 12 to 27 percent were from other backward classes.[41] These are the lowest people in the Indian social class structure.

Dowry: too high a price to pay. Traditionally, in India, a bride's family pays a sum of money—called a *dowry*—to the groom. Payments may continue well into the marriage, upon demand by the husband's family. (These payments are taken quite seriously, as proved by frequent reports in India of "dowry killings," in which a husband murders his wife in retaliation for nonpayment of dowry.) The amount of a dowry can reach into the hundreds or thousands of dollars, equaling months, if not years, of income for a poor or middle-income family. Dowries, therefore, are a tremendous burden on families with marriageable girls.

The dowry system contributes to child prostitution both directly and indirectly. Parents hoping to avoid paying a dowry may choose, instead of marrying off their daughter, to dedicate her as a religious prostitute or simply to sell her to a brothel keeper. Even earlier, as a preemptive measure, they may choose to kill a daughter shortly after birth or (more likely) to abort her before she is born, so as not to have to raise a dowry for her later. "The unholy alliance between tradition (son complex) and technology (ultrasound) has created havoc in Indian society: some families see it as more desirable to spend a few thousand rupees on pre-natal sex determination tests and sex selective abortions, than to spend hundreds of thousands of rupees on, dowry later on."[42] One result of this shortage in available brides is the trafficking of women and girls into prostitution in order to satisfy men's demand for sex.

It is tragic that a tradition of bride payment should lead to the loss of life and liberty for so many young girls.

Females as second-class citizens. India has made notable efforts to improve the status of women within its borders. In 1985 the Indian government formed the Department of Women and Child Development, and it has passed numerous acts making men and women equal before the law. Still, the view of women remains low in much of India, with direct repercussions for the prostitution of women and girls.

One indication of how poorly females are viewed in Indian society is to realize how few of them (comparatively) there are. According to the latest Indian census, the female-to-male gender ratio is 933 females for every 1,000 males, dropping to a distribution as low as 722 girls for every 1,000 boys in some rural areas.[43] There are fewer females, in part, because girls and women have higher mortality rates due to greater poverty and more limited access to good nutrition and health care. As we have seen, the gender imbalance is also partly due to gender-based abortion and female infanticide by parents who wanted sons rather than daughters.[44]

Other facts back up the low status of women. The Asian Development Bank states, "India invests far less in its women workers than in its working men. Women also receive a smaller share of what society produces: they are less endowed than men with health care, education, and productive assets that could increase their return to labor. Women's nutritional levels are lower than men's; more women than men die before the age of thirty-five. Three fourths of Indian women are illiterate. Some 90 percent of rural and 70 percent of urban women workers are unskilled."[45]

In such an environment of discrimination against females, it is not surprising that parents will listen when a brothel keeper offers them a handful of rupees to put their daughter in a brothel. After all, she's just a girl.

The devadasi system—religious prostitution. To many Westerners, religious prostitution might seem as outdated as the Canaanite practices condemned in the Hebrew Scriptures. Yet religious prostitution is alive and well in India today, and the girls caught up in this system often find themselves taking the next step into ordinary prostitution.

The districts bordering Maharashtra and Karnataka states in west-central India— where Restore International has thus far been most active— are known as the "devadasi belt." In the devadasi system, girls as young as six are dedicated to a god or goddess, going through a marriage ceremony that will prevent them from marrying a man later and that commits them to fulfilling the sexual desire of any man who wants them. This special religious status, though now illegal, still exists and in the minds of many justifies putting a girl into prostitution.

We will look at this route into prostitution in much more detail in the following chapter, as it well illustrates the combination of cultural forces that can put a girl into brothel servitude.

Fatalism. Hinduism, the dominant religion in India, is a collection of tremendously diverse religious beliefs and practices.[46] One of the ideas generally accepted by Hindus is that of *samsara,* or reincarnation—the idea that each person experiences a long series of physical births, deaths, and rebirths. Meanwhile, *karma* is the law that every action, thought, and decision has a consequence, for good or ill, that will redound upon the person in this life or in a future one. Thus, if we are experiencing hardship, it means that we did something in our earlier years, or in a past life, to deserve it.

This philosophy breeds an attitude of fatalism. A girl who finds herself trafficked into prostitution might easily think, *This is the way it has to be.* Others might think about her, *She deserves no better than to work in a brothel. After all, her own karma made her an outcaste.* Or they might think, *Well, her life is hard, but maybe in her next life she'll have it easier. There's no point in trying to help her.*

We can't ignore the role religious fatalism plays in leading many to accept the existence of child prostitution instead of seeking to eradicate it. It's a part of the culture that permits child rape to continue.

Other causes. Along with the causes of child prostitution described above, others contribute to the problem as well. These include both society-wide causes and personal causes within the lives and homes of the prostitutes.

Changes in the economy can be especially hard on the poor and uneducated, thus encouraging some girls to go into prostitution. Industrialization has made some manual trades obsolete. Globalization has taken a toll on traditional livelihoods, such as subsistence agriculture and cottage crafts. Urbanization has driven village youngsters to seek a better life in the cities. Materialism has caused people increasingly to desire consumer goods and to be willing to do whatever it takes to get the money for what they want.

Victim Profile: Reshmi

Reshmi is from Mudhol, a town about seventy miles southeast of the city of Kolhapur. [48] Her father, Shashidhar, died five years ago. Her mother, Inayat, does housework for a living. She has two sisters. Reshmi is between seventeen and nineteen years old and is a devadasi. Reshmi has never been to school, but primarily speaks Kannada and understands some Hindi and Marathi.

In her village she worked with her mother doing housework. While working, she met a friend named Sahila. When Reshmi shared with Sahila about her financial problems, Sahila introduced her to the profession of prostitution. Sahila brought Reshmi to her home in Gokul Nagar, Sangli, three years ago, employing her to do housework. Sahila was a prostitute who had two houses, one her residence (where Reshmi lived with her) and the other a place of business. After working for Sahila for a month doing housework, Reshmi decided to join Sahila in prostitution because she thought she would make more money. Two months later, Sahila died. Reshmi returned Sahila's and her residence to Bharati, the owner.

(cont'd on next page)

Social and legal conditions can also contribute to child prostitution. India's immigration policies are inadequate to deal with cross-border trafficking. Its economic policies, while well-intended, have not enabled India's growing wealth to spread widely to its people. Poor governance has meant that anti-trafficking laws and mandated rehabilitation measures have not been implemented consistently in all of the nation's states and union territories. The central government's failure to curb discriminatory practices against lower castes, ethnic minorities, and tribal communities has helped to ensure that an exploitative, prostitution-favoring culture remains in place.

From my personal experience, I must say that the most appalling cause of sex trafficking is the lack of adequate enforcement of India laws. Corrupt officers may be customers of the minor children, may take bribes to tip off the brothel owners with information that a raid will occur, may allow minor girls to cross the borders into other states and countries, or may be unknowledgeable as to how to enforce the laws prohibiting sex trafficking. If the Indian police were consistently doing their job, and were enforcing the laws that are on the books, the child prostitution problem would shrink to a tiny vestige of its current dimension.

Meanwhile, on a more personal scale, individual and family problems make certain girls more vulnerable to prostitution than are others. Girls who were born with disabilities or disfigurement, whose birth families have broken up, who have low self-esteem, who have married young and are abused or deserted by their husbands, who have been victims of physical or sexual abuse, who are drug abusers, or who have family members involved in commercial sexual exploitation are all more likely to wind up as prostitutes.[47] Their personal disadvantages have united with larger social problems to condemn them to a life of sexual degradation.

Consequences of Child Prostitution

Sex trafficking has a wide-ranging damaging effect. Not only can it lead to a legacy of sex trafficking spiraling down from one generation to the next, but also it leaves permanent scars on the trafficked young girl, her family, and her society.

The negative consequences begin where the trafficking itself often begins: in the home. When parents sell their children to brothel owners, the sanctity of the family is violated. The young girls are betrayed by their families, dissolving their trusting relationships.

Prostitution violates the dignity of the young girls. Even after the girls are rescued, they may not want to return home, because they will no longer be accepted by their family or their community. This may cause the rescued girls to revert back into prostitution, as they have nowhere else to turn.

They will carry their past histories of continuous rapes, beatings, imprisonment, and threats with them throughout the rest of their lives through haunting memories, resulting in lower self-esteem and affecting their decisions. As one report put it,

> The mental and emotional state of the survivors may include malevolence, helplessness and withdrawal; disassociation; self-blame and identification with the aggressor; distraction; a foreshortened view of time; normalisation and shaping,

She continued to live in the other room and meet customers there, paying Bharati 300 rupees (about $6.75) in rent. Although Reshmi remained in prostitution in order to support her family, she was unable to send any money home to them, because her income of 50 rupees per customer (having two customers per day) was equal to her expenses.

Having been in Sangli for three years at the time we interviewed her, she is ready to return home and to work there, though she is unsure of what she can do. She does not want to return to prostitution, despite feeling that she did right by engaging in the profession because it was her only means of livelihood. Additionally, she is unsure of whether her mother will be effective in keeping her away from prostitution.

Sex Work and Death by AIDS

The HIV infection rate in the Indian population is believed to be slightly below 1 percent. Viewed strictly as a percentage, that figure might seem low, but in such a populous nation, it represents millions of persons affected by the disease. Officially, there are 5.1 million Indians infected with HIV,[50] putting India behind only South Africa, with its 5.3 million infections. But does that tell the true story?

"The official statistics are wrong. India is in first place," says Richard Feachem, executive director of the Global Fund to Fight AIDS, Tuberculosis and Malaria. "The epidemic [in India] is growing very rapidly. It is out of control. There is nothing happening in India today that is big or serious enough to prevent it."[51]

Feachem most likely is right. India is one of five countries that were classified by the U.S. National Intelligence Council in 2002 as representing the second wave of the worldwide HIV/AIDS epidemic.[52]

Projections put the number of HIV-infected persons in India at from between 9 and 25 million people by the year 2010.[53]

(cont'd on next page)

whereby the victims convince themselves that their experiences had to happen instead of viewing them as traumatic. ... Some of the psychiatric disorders among survivors of trafficking are listed as post-traumatic stress disorder, depressive disorder, dissociative disorders, psychotic disorders and eating disorders. ...

Since such psychological trauma usually remains unaddressed and unresolved, "the abused turn into abusers," ... with a high probability of them becoming criminals.[49]

Sex trafficking murders its victims. Forced to have sex with as many as twenty customers per day at the command of the brothel owners, the young girls are at a high risk of contracting a deadly disease, such as HIV/AIDS. Once they are diagnosed, they may be forced out onto the streets, left to take care of themselves. If a young girl fails to cooperate with the brothel owner and refuses to entertain customers, or if she attempts to run away, she may be severely beaten or killed. Rather than living in the conditions she was sold into, the young victim of sex trafficking may resort to suicide.

Sex trafficking also fuels the breakdown of society. Trafficking perpetuates patriarchal attitudes, which in turn undermine efforts to eradicate discrimination against women and girls. It infringes upon human rights and fuels crime. The more the police fail to react responsibly to the problem of sex trafficking, the more normal and acceptable it becomes. Sex trafficking hinders India's development, as the economy is driven by commercial sex rather than legal businesses. As bribes are accepted from the brothel owners, India's government is disrupted. Sex trafficking prevents the young girl from receiving an education, keeping her from contributing to her society in a positive way.

Measures of child prostitution's costs, then, cannot be taken only in terms of rupees. The personal and social expense comes to a far greater sum than any monetary amount ever could. The great nation of India bleeds from this wound—and will continue to do so until something is done to heal her.

What Is Being Done—and Can Be Done

The government of India deserves credit for recognizing the problem of child prostitution within its borders and for at least making attempts to eradicate it. At the same time, the continued presence of this terrible form of slavery among the Karishmas of the land cries out for a stronger, more effective response.

The main government body attempting to prevent sex trafficking and protect trafficking victims is the Department of Women and Child Development (DWCD).[57] In 1998 the DWCD formulated a nationwide action plan to combat trafficking and the commercial sexual exploitation of women and girls. The plan covered various strategies, such as prevention, awareness raising, economic empowerment, rescue, and rehabilitation. This plan has been criticized at a number of points, but at least the DWCD has been trying to take some action.

Legally, India has taken a firm stand against sex trafficking. It is a signatory to, or sponsor of, laws and conventions at many different levels. India has agreed to important international concords such as the UN's Protocol to Prevent, Suppress and Punish Trafficking in Persons, Especially Women and Children

India is quickly becoming the center of gravity for the worldwide AIDS epidemic. And the situation for sex workers is far worse than that among the general population of India. According to UN statistics, among sex workers in urban areas, the HIV infection rate is around 52 percent, while in rural areas, sex workers are infected at a rate of about 30 percent. [54] Moreover, the epidemic is spreading fastest in India among sex workers, especially in populous southern states such as Maharashtra. What all this means is that, given enough time in the flesh business, a girl has a very high chance of contracting HIV/AIDS.

But, it may not even take much time to become infected with the deadly disease. As we have seen, in many cases, men who have HIV/AIDS will actually seek out young girls and have unprotected sex with them, mistakenly believing that this will cure them. This is the worst possible thing that could happen to a young girl's health. It has cost thousands of girls their lives.

Surveys have shown that the great majority of prostitutes in India are aware of HIV/AIDS.

(cont'd on next page)

Among them, however, only about three-quarters report taking regular preventive measures. Many of those girls and women who have contracted HIV are pressured by their bosses to keep their health status secret, thereby increasing the spread of the disease.[55] Or else they are thrown out of the brothel, cast upon a society that has little use for them.

Compounding the problem of HIV infection among minors in prostitution is the discrimination that these unfortunates often face because of their HIV status. Human Rights Watch, in its report "Future Forsaken," has documented the ways that Indian children affected by HIV/AIDS are segregated in society and hindered from getting adequate health care, such as by being refused antiretroviral treatment. Child prostitutes, as well as the children of prostitutes, are among the most vulnerable to such discriminatory treatment.[56] Insult is added to injury, and death comes that much sooner.

(2000),[58] as well as to regional instruments such as the SAARC Convention on Preventing and Combating the Trafficking in Women and Children for Prostitution (2002). India's own Constitution outlaws trafficking in persons,[59] while the Indian Penal Code defines guidelines and sentences for trafficking.[60] The central government's specific laws relating to child prostitution include the Immoral Traffic (Prevention) Act (1956)[61] and the Juvenile Justice Act (1986).[62] There are also some state legal instruments bearing on the problem, such as the Goa Children's Act (2003).

Signing laws is one thing; getting the problem fixed is another. The fact is, the problem of child prostitution in India is not going away and may even be getting worse year by year. The anti-trafficking laws and conventions are not being effectively enforced, and thus the nation has convicted relatively few offenders and only rarely shuts down trafficking networks. And this is the reason that India bears the onus of being placed on the U.S. State Department's Tier 2 Special Watch List. According to the State Department, "The Government of India does not fully comply with the minimum standards for the elimination of trafficking. ... India is placed on the Tier 2 Watch List for the third consecutive year due to its failure to show evidence of increasing efforts to address trafficking in persons."[63]

India is a poor country with limited resources and a lot of problems that it needs to address simultaneously, child prostitution being only one of them. The massive bureaucracy of the government hinders effective action. Meanwhile, corruption or at least incompetence in law enforcement, the legislatures, and even the judiciary is nearly endemic. For reasons such as these, too little progress is being made despite the good intentions and hard work of some. Will the leaders of the nation be able to make a difference? We hope so and we wait to see it.

One of the most hopeful signs is India's general willingness to work with nongovernmental organizations (NGOs) and community-based organizations (CBOs). In fact, in many ways, the NGOs and CBOs are taking the lead in combating child prostitution in India. They are the ones who know what is really going on at a local level and are willing to intervene with prevention, rescue, and rehabilitation. It is reasonable to hope that, over time, such organizations can enliven the Indian police forces and courts to do their job and to at last turn the tide against child sexual exploitation.

My colleagues and I are committed in various places in the world to staying involved in the difficult and often unpleasant work of going into the brothels, finding underage girls kept against their will and against the law, and pulling them out to set them on the road to a better life lived in freedom. We have no illusions about this work being easy. Getting it done demands people who are willing not to just talk about doing it, but to get out and do it on a regular basis. As a result, organizationally, we have experienced the relational stress and strain associated with demanding no less than people sold out to *doing*. Nevertheless, we continue to find people who are willing to go places they need to go to find and rescue the kids.

We know there will be setbacks. We know it can be tricky to make any advances we accomplish really stick. We are all acutely aware of our own failings and limitations and know we all walk with a limp. So we extend grace and applause to everyone courageous enough to be a part of the fight. After all, as we have seen in this chapter, the problem is a huge one. The work is demanding and we are up against a problem deeply entrenched in Indian and other societies around the world. But, we believe that perseverance, determination, and faith can work wonders in even the worst situations.

We constantly remind ourselves about how Jesus modeled going after "the one." Karishma was one of the "ones," and she and her sisters around the globe are worth it.

FOUR
A Necklace of Beads

The Devadasi Route into Child Prostitution

Sattyava was a thirteen-year-old village girl when one day an "Auntie" she didn't know came to her house and spoke with her parents. This woman offered to find a job for Sattyava in a town more than a hundred miles away.

"My parents jumped at the opportunity," recalled Sattyava. "Money was scarce, and I was a burden to them. They had dedicated me to the goddess Yellamma when I was six, and as a result, I was forbidden to marry. How could I know that this dedication meant a future of forced prostitution?"

When Sattyava got to her new town, "Auntie" sold her to an old woman for twelve thousand rupees (about three hundred dollars). "Auntie" then left and the old lady said to Sattyava, "Now you must have sex with men every day until you have earned what you cost."

"No!" she screamed. "Never."

A pimp came in and beat Sattyava. Starved and isolated until she submitted to her new work, she was required to have sex with men at least five times per night.

After a few months of this, a different kind of man showed up and paid to spend a few minutes with her. Not touching her, he asked her about herself and assured her that she would soon be out of her imprisonment. The next night, police raided the brothel and Sattyava was freed.

Sadly, the only thing unusual about Satyavva's story is the fact that she was rescued from her brothel captivity in the end. Certainly her first step toward prostitution—dedication by her parents as a devadasi—is common enough in South India.[1] In our interviews of girls rescued from brothels, typically more than half of them identify themselves as being a devadasi.

Looking into this uniquely Indian status for a young girl can help us understand how religious, social, and economic influences can combine to sentence her to a life of sexual servitude.

An Ancient Tradition

No country has a more diverse and complex religious makeup than India. And amid all the gods, festivals, and rituals of the land, one relatively obscure—and in the modern era illegal—religious practice persists in certain rural areas of South India. This is the practice of a dedicating a young girl or boy (usually a girl) to a god or a goddess. The child dedication practice, as it exists today, is the debased vestige of an ancient tradition within Hinduism.

Most often the deity to whom a girl like Satyavva is dedicated is the goddess Yellamma, a favorite among Dalits (outcaste Indians, or "untouchables"), who seek her protection. Sometimes, though, dedications are made to others deities, including the popular monkey god Hanuman. The title of the dedicatee varies, depending upon where she lives. Many of these girls are known as *devadasis*, a Sanskrit term meaning "handmaidens of the goddess," but they might also be termed *joginis, jogathis, basivis, matammas, venkatasanis,* or something else. The boy dedicatees, who are forced to become transvestites, are often called *jogappas*.

The practice of child dedication is believed to have begun around the sixth century A.D. and many myths are offered to explain how it started. According to one of these myths, a Brahman father ordered his son to kill the son's mother. When the son obeyed by decapitating his mother, the father gave him three wishes as his reward. With his first wish, the son brought his mother back to life. Since the mother's head could not be found, the head of a lower-caste woman named Yellamma was attached to the mother's body. In this way, a lower-caste woman achieved the higher status of becoming a Brahman's wife. And after this, lower-caste girls started being dedicated to the goddess Yellamma.[2]

Regardless of its actual origins, the practice of child dedication grew in popularity as temple-based worship flourished in India. The practice reached its peak in the tenth and eleventh centuries, when wealthy temples had as many four hundred devadasis attached to them as celibate temple dancers. After that period, the devadasi system began to decline as invaders from West Asia penetrated India and destroyed numerous temples. By the time the British arrived, the devadasi system was all but extinct in North India, though it maintained a stubborn presence in the South.

As little as one hundred years ago, devadasis were still treated with some respect and provided with an adequate living. Since then, however, the system has become more abusive as the temples that sheltered devadasis have lost their wealth and the devadasis' temple endowments have been confiscated. The primary role of devadasis went from being temple dancers to being prostitutes, and the status of these women has correspondingly dropped. Devadasis today are usually destitute, uneducated women who receive little or no support from the temples they serve and who are expected to satisfy the lust of any man who wants them.

Attitudes toward the devadasi system are split between those who want to reform it and those who want to eliminate it.

During the early twentieth century, reformers led by members of the Theosophical Society of India wanted to return devadasis to their earlier status as temple dancers. Theosophist pioneers Madame Blavatsky (1831–91) and Henry Olcott (1832–1907), as well as a later leader of the group, Annie Besant (1847–1933), tried to restore various forms of sacred dance in India, including devadasi dances, as a means of lifting people up to a higher spiritual plane.

Today there is no organized campaign to revive and reform the devadasi system, but the system still has many who are willing to defend it, at least in part. Some of them are devadasis themselves who would like an improved economic and social status for their group, but who criticize anyone who looks down on them or refers to them simplistically as prostitutes. Nevertheless, the weight of public opinion and political decision has fallen heavily on the side of eliminating the devadasi system.

The first anti-dedication movement was started in 1882, led by missionaries, doctors, journalists, and social workers. The movement first concentrated on building public opinion against devadasi practices, but by the end of the nineteenth century, it had turned into an attempt to abolish the devadasi system outright. Such prominent social reformers as Isvar Chandra Vidyasagar (1820–91) and Mahadev Govind Ranade (1842–1901) lent their voices in support of abolishing the devadasi system. The tide of public opinion in India began to turn, and those within the abolition movement welcomed legislative solutions to the problem.

Both during British rule and since India's independence in 1947, legislators in India have enacted laws to prevent the dedication of children to deities. In 1924, for instance, the Indian Penal Code was amended to add sections 372 and 373, outlawing the buying and selling of minors for purposes of prostitution. This, in effect, made the prostitution aspect of child dedication illegal.[3] The first specific legal initiative to outlaw the devadasi system was the Bombay Devadasi Protection Act of 1934, pertaining to the Bombay province as it existed under the British Raj. The act made dedication of females illegal, whether consensual or not. A violation of the act would subject a person to a year in prison, a fine, or both. The act also instituted marriage and property rights for devadasis and their children.

In 1947 the Madras Devadasi Prevention of Dedication Act outlawed dedication in the southern province now known as Karnataka. This act and the Bombay act were both replaced by the Karnataka Devadasis (Prohibition of Dedication) Act in 1982. This act declared the practice of child dedication to be illegal and imposed sentences for offenders. Under the act, persons who are guilty of dedicating a child to a deity and who are not related to that child are liable to paying a fine and serving up to three years in prison. Parents, guardians, and relatives face stiffer punishment: they are to pay a fine and serve not less than two years nor more than five years for dedicating a child to a deity. Importantly, the Karnataka act provided for rules to be adopted to care for, protect, and rehabilitate devadasis. In Andhra Pradesh, a similar act was adopted in 1988.

Despite all efforts opposing it, however, the devadasi system has not yet died out. Estimates of the number of devadasis in Andhra Pradesh State alone range as high as forty-two thousand. An estimated five thousand to fifteen thousand children are dedicated each year. The devadasis are almost all members of the lowest castes—95 percent belong to the scheduled castes (Mala and Madiga) and scheduled tribes, while a small percentage belong to the backward castes, such as the Telaga and Chakali. In a case study of eighty-five devadasis belonging to Yellampura village, one researcher found not a single upper-caste woman dedicated to the deity. The devadasi practice was being followed by the lower castes such as the Holers, Madars, and Samagars.[4] Most devadasis live in Maharashtra, Karnataka, and Andhra Pradesh states—all in South India.

The majority of devadasis have monthly incomes of no more than 1,000 rupees (approximately $22.50). According to one study, 95 percent of them are illiterate. The children of devadasis have no property rights with their fathers and thus have little hope of climbing out of poverty. Most daughters of devadasis become devadasis themselves. Due to poverty and deprivation, as well as HIV/AIDS, few devadasis live past the age of fifty, and often their life expectancy is much lower. Unless a devadasi has a son who is willing to bury her, her corpse is likely to be left out in the open to be eaten by dogs and other animals.

The devadasi's existence is hardly a life anyone would objectively desire for herself, yet it's one that many a girl is sentenced to at an early age.

Married to Yellamma

Satyavva was dedicated when she was six, and that was only slightly younger than the typical age of from eight to ten. At such a tender age, a girl goes through a marriage ceremony—most likely the only one she will ever have. Afterward, she is considered to be married to a deity or to a temple, and she is supposed to marry no man. In fact, it is believed that if she were later to marry, she would bring misfortune upon herself, her husband, and her entire village. She is a devadasi for life.

There are a number of reasons why a parent might choose to dedicate a young child as a devadasi.

Sometimes the motive is genuinely religious, or at least superstitious. Perhaps the girl's father was healed from a sickness and he wants to thank the gods by dedicating his daughter. In some places, if a girl has copper-colored hair (a result of malnourishment) or matted hair (caused by poor hygiene), it is considered to be a summons by the goddess Yellamma. Sometimes a sick girl child is left outside a temple to Yellamma, and if she is still alive in the morning, it is believed that she was born to serve the goddess. Nirmala Grace, leader of an anti-devadasi organization, says that for many Indian families "dedicating a young child is like submitting a tender bud to god. It is the ultimate offering in worship."[5]

Most times, though, the motivation is more mercenary. Parents might want to get rid of a daughter who was born with a disability, might desire to avoid paying her dowry, or might look forward to receiving money when they sell their daughter into prostitution. Since, unlike other girls, devadasis are permitted to inherit their parents' property, families who have no sons might choose to dedicate one of their daughters as a devadasi so that she can serve as a surrogate "son" and keep the property in the family. Sometimes an older devadasi will go into a trance during a festival and then claim that she has received a revelation from Yellamma that a certain girl is supposed to be dedicated to her. This "trance" was induced not by the goddess, but by a wealthy patron of a temple who wanted the girl for sex and paid for the trance to occur. The parents don't know this, and so they go along with the dedication.

The dedication ceremony varies from place to place, but in general it is modeled on the type of wedding ceremony used by Brahmans (members of the highest caste). In fact, the ceremony is often paid for by a wealthy Brahman male who by doing so purchases sexual access to the girl once she reaches puberty. Sometimes the Brahman will make arrangements directly with the temple priests, and sometimes he will negotiate with the girl's parents using a senior devadasi as a go-between.

The ceremony is held at the time of the full moon on a Tuesday or a Friday—the two days of the week considered most auspicious for the worship of female deities. Traditionally, it has been held at a temple of the goddess, though in recent years the ceremony has often been held in a home in order for the participants to avoid prosecution under India's anti-dedication laws. In any case, the ceremony location is first ritually cleansed with water and cow dung. Then five measures of nine different powders are spread out before an image of the goddess in a special design. To complete the preparation, four pots filled with oil are placed at the four corners of the design and lamps are lit.

During the ceremony, there is (of course) no groom; a picture of the goddess takes his place. Family members of the girl and others in the community show up to participate in the feasting and drinking that will follow the ceremony. While those in attendance sing songs of praise to Yellamma, thread is wound through the pots and then tied to the little girl's neck. This symbolizes her attachment to Yellamma and to Yellamma's temple. Next, the priest comes up to the girl with a necklace of white or red beads in his hand, similar to the *talis*, or string necklace that married women throughout India wear to indicate their marital status. He asks a few questions of those dedicating the girl, then turns to her and gives her instructions for her new life as a devadasi.

The priest says to the young girl, "You cannot be the wife of any man. You must fast on Tuesday and Friday, begging with a *joga* [begging bowl made of bamboo cane] in your hand. You must visit at least five houses when doing so. If you happen to see a calf suckling its mother, you may not pull the calf away. If a cow grazes the crop before you, you must not drive it away. You may not speak untruth. If you are feeling hungry, don't tell others this, but ask them for food. Offer shelter to the homeless and to strangers. Provide food to the hungry and water to the thirsty. Help the helpless. If anybody abuses you or beats you, do not retaliate. If you come across a corpse, take a bath and visit the temple of Yellamma. Do not eat until you have worshiped the goddess. Do not eat somebody else's leftover food. Chant glory to Yellamma all the time."

After his speech, the priest ties the bead necklace to the girl's neck, symbolizing her marriage to Yellamma just as in the West putting on a ring symbolizes marriage. The priest also sets a begging bowl on the girl's head. With the *joga* on her head, she walks through the village, where upper-caste people bow before her. With the older devadasis singing in a line behind her, she visits at least five homes to beg.

She is now a member of the cult of Yellamma.

The Life of a Devadasi

After dedication, a young girl goes back to her parents' home and for a while her life resumes its previous course. When she reaches puberty, a second stage of her initiation occurs and she then enters more fully into the life of a devadasi. This second stage is marked by ritual ceremonies that are less elaborate than her earlier "marriage" ceremony. It is capped by her deflowering by a priest or (more likely these days) by a wealthy Brahman who has paid for the privilege. The idea is that the deity, through her surrogate, has consummated the marriage and the girl must now begin her service as the deity's bride.

In her new life as an active devadasi, a girl will each morning take a bath and present herself at the temple of Yellamma. In most cases, she is not permitted to enter the temple, so she bows from outside. She then sweeps the temple grounds. Other devadasis teach her how to perform their dances and perhaps how to play a stringed instrument for accompaniment.

Some of the time, a devadasi carries a metal vessel or a bamboo basket, called a *jaga*, on her head containing a bust of Yellamma. (The members of her cult believe that their deity's blessing makes it possible for them to balance a basket on their head without any other support.) The basket is decorated with flowers or brightly colored cloth. A devadasi may even dance with the basket and bust of Yellamma on her head.

Every Tuesday and Friday, the devadasi goes around her village, carrying a slate in her hands saying that she is a devadasi and begging for food. Historically, during weddings, funerals, and religious fairs, she was invited to bless the event. A devadasi would keep a fast when there

A Blessing That Was a Curse

For five hundred years, the town of Mahbubnagar in Andhra Pradesh State has held an annual festival called Polepalli Jatara. Traditionally, the highlight of the festival would begin with tying a naked devadasi to a wicker basket and hoisting her up in the air at the end of a 120-foot pole. The wicker basket, with the devadasi inside, would then be rotated, and the devadasi (supposed to represent the goddess Yellamma in the flesh) would shower vermilion and flowers on the crowd below as a blessing. On the ground, other devadasis would be dancing and the crowd would be having a good time, but meanwhile, up above, the "living goddess" was being spun around so rapidly that she often suffered broken ribs and in some years even died. Her reward (if she survived) was a few rupees and a bottle of liquor.

This long-standing ritual of "blessing" in Mahbubnagar illustrates the kind of cruelty and humiliation with which devadasis are all too often served. Thankfully, after protests by women's organizations, the state government in 2001 passed a resolution against this ritual and it has not been practiced since.

was a death in a family. When she was invited to a wedding, she would walk along with the groom and bride around the *pandal* (large tent put up for special events). She smears turmeric and vermilion on her forehead for special occasions and participates with other devadasis in performing intricate religious dances.

At least twice a year she is expected to visit the Yellamma shrine on full moon days to confirm her obedience to the goddess. Traditionally, during this semiannual ritual, she was expected to be nude or at most to cover her body with foliage from the sacred neem tree. Since in recent years these religious events have become attractions for voyeurs, today a devadasi is more likely to wear clothing at these events. Still, the events can involve lewd dancing as the women contort themselves into erotic positions.

One devadasi, named Parvathi, recalled her first humiliating dances. "I was about thirteen," she says. "I had to dance for five or six hours a day for two weeks. The men would tease me, call out and ask me to do sexual moves. The whole village was there and the women would watch and call out, too. Even my friends made fun of me. I felt so ashamed and shy."[6]

As we can see from the devadasi's activities, she is supposed to serve the temple of Yellamma as well as the community in general. Another way in which she is supposed to serve others is by satisfying the sexual urges of men. She is not permitted to marry anyone, since she is already "married" to the goddess, but she is expected to have sex with men. As with all the other aspects of being a devadasi, if a girl refuses to cooperate with the sexual requirement of her status, she will be rejected by her family and her village.

It is the sexual aspect of a devadasi's life that has come to greater prominence in recent years within the devadasi system and that has led to so many girls becoming prostitutes.[7]

Descent into Prostitution

A devadasi's sexual exploitation begins at puberty with the second stage of her introduction into the devadasi system when she is deflowered—or to put it plainly, raped—by a priest or by one of the local landlords. The "suitor" need not have any personal connection with the temple. He cannot, however, be a Muslim or a Christian. Neither can he be a member of one of the lower castes; he can only be a Brahman or a member of one of the other upper castes. (Clearly, a large measure of social prejudice informs the devadasi system.) Since members of the upper castes normally have the most wealth, this provision ensures that more money will make its way into the hands of temple priests and the girl's parents.

After the initial rape, the girl is considered to belong to the temple patron who first paid for her. As long as he pays to maintain her, or until he becomes bored with her, she is his (though she may be expected to sleep with other men as well). Usually she remains his concubine for a period of months, perhaps years. As soon as he loses interest in her, he may discard her with no further responsibility for her or her children.

This is when the most difficult part of her journey begins. Once she is dropped by her patron—usually while she is still a young teenager—she becomes the common property of the men where she lives. If she is to fulfill her religious duty to satisfy men, she will let them sleep with her whenever they ask, accepting only a hundred rupees in return. In essence, she has become an ordinary prostitute.

"I used to cry when men started doing strange things to me when I was very young," one devadasi named Jayshree Ranaya reported. "I was with one priest for five years and after he got married I had to go with different men. I had no choice. I started begging and living on the streets of Belgaum."[8]

Not all devadasis become prostitutes, but more than 40 percent do. The rest do agricultural work or perform other manual labor to support themselves and their families. Less than 3 percent of them marry.

A devadasi who enters prostitution may stay in her own village to practice her "profession." More likely, though, she will move to one of the larger cities and work at a brothel, perhaps one owned by an older devadasi.

Indeed, in many places, the appearance of senior devadasis at certain seasons of the year to procure new girls for the brothels is expected. They show up well dressed and spreading money around. They do this to gain favor in the community and also as a way of saying, "See how much money you can make if you go into prostitution?"

Sometimes a devadasi girl enters prostitution because she thinks she has no other option. At other times her parents or other relatives will sell her to a pimp or brothel keeper, just as Satyavva was sold for $300. Such a sum may seem small to us, but it represents a significant fee in a poor village of India.

One researcher into India's religious prostitution has stated, "It is not true that all girls willingly agree to become divine prostitutes and go to brothels."

> Like other girls, they too would like to marry, if possible, the man of their liking, and have a family and children of their own. This dream they get by seeing other well-settled girls in their own caste and village. They also resist the offer [to become a prostitute], since they have seen the fate of other divine prostitutes in the village. Some have learnt this from the experience of their own sisters or cousins. But their parents pressurize them, tempt them and plead with them to go and help their family monetarily. Sometimes, they are asked to sacrifice their comforts and dreams for the good of their younger sisters, and brothers who are to be married. They plead their inability to protect them against the dominant personalities in the community, who will in any case get them by hook or crook. Ultimately the girls yield to persuasion, threats, temptations.[9]

Brothel keepers like to have devadasis in their *dhabas* because the devadasis' status as religious functionaries makes them less likely to be arrested and tried for prostitution. And this makes them more profitable to their brothels. (It also encourages perpetuation of the devadasi system.)[10] And so, in certain red-light areas, devadasis are prevalent. Almost 80 percent of prostitutes in major towns of Maharashtra are devadasis.[11]

The devadasi system, thus, often becomes like a chute for the girls who are thrown into it. They slide down, down, down until they reach the bottom—bargain-basement prostitutes in a large city like Mumbai or a smaller city like Sangli. It's at the bottom where we have tried to scoop up Satyavva and her sisters and restore life to them. We attempt to pull them out of the sexual servitude where they have ended up and try to give them a new life for which their devadasi background has done little to prepare them. A new life of freedom, hope, and dignity.

The Future of the Devadasi System

Only a few people have been convicted under the Devadasi Act. The practice appears to be continuing the slow decline that began a thousand years ago, but it is still far from extinct. Those who benefit from it carry on with it in the supposedly enlightened twenty-first century, just not as much in the public eye as before.

Efforts are being made to bring the reality into conformity with the legal requirements. For example, a collective of former devadasis in Andhra Pradesh works in some five hundred villages, talking to parents about why they should not dedicate their daughters and shaming men into not starting sexual relationships with vulnerable girls. Ranjan, a member of the collective, said, "We tell these girls they can have another life. We inform them about government loans to which they are entitled—each rehabilitated jogini [devadasi] is eligible for 10,000 rupees, which will pay them interest of 100 rupees or £1.50 a month. They can supplement this with agricultural labour. And, they can also claim housing loans sponsored by the government. But, unless we tell them about this, nobody knows."[12]

As Ranjan alludes to, governments in India are trying to make devadasis less economically dependent as an encouragement for them to leave their tradition of prostitution. The Maharashtra state government, for example, gives a monthly pension of 300 rupees to devadasis over the age of forty and financial assistance of 10,000 rupees for the marriage of a devadasi or the daughter of a devadasi.

At Restore International, we support every effort to end the devadasi system. Adequate laws are already in place; what are needed now are more efforts like those of the collective referred to above to draw attention to the problems inherent in the devadasi system and to encourage enforcement of the laws. If parents refuse to endanger their daughters, if priests stop acting as procurers for pedophiles, if police arrest those who carry out prostitution of underage girls, the devadasi exploitation of children will come to an end at long last. And good riddance.

Certainly we affirm the right of the people of India and every other country to worship as they wish—but not at the expense of girls too young and defenseless to choose the sort of life they are being inducted into. And besides, let's be frank about what is happening here: money, not religion, is what's really fueling the devadasi system. There's a market for sex with young girls, and priests, parents, and pimps are all willing to take away a young girl's freedom—and eventually her life—in order to get their hands on some of that money. If a religious institution exists that makes it easier for them to sell girls, then they'll take advantage of it. That's just wrong.

Of course, if the devadasi system were to be eradicated tomorrow, that would not end the trafficking of girls into the flesh trade. But, it would close off one of the major pipelines supplying the brothels of Mumbai and other cities around India. We would find fewer Satyavvas when we go in to rescue girls.

The battle against the devadasi system illustrates what it will take to change millennia-old customs in India that contribute to the exploitation and enslavement of children. It's a battle that must be waged unremittingly on every front. My nongovernmental organization, Restore International, and the team of staff and volunteers who are working in India are determined to do just that.

PART TWO:

Restore International

FIVE

A New Combatant in the War on Slavery

The Birth of Restore International

It was shortly after 8:00 P.M. on October 21, 2005, and my colleague and I were in the city of Sangli, India, waiting inside a white SUV with our driver, Rajiv. Parked a short distance outside the Sangli red-light district of Gokul Nagar, we were serving as backup for our investigator Pranit Mayakunar and two others, who had entered the brothel area just minutes before. Restore International had done a raid with the police in the same red-light area that year, leading to many young girls being released and many brothel owners and their thugs being arrested. The red-light area was still white-hot with anger that we had infiltrated the brothels in May and uncovered the existence of more than seventeen young girls who were held captive. The brothel owners were further undone that the police (with whom they seemingly had an arrangement) were no longer turning a blind eye to their illegal activities, but were willing to deal them a crushing blow.

We decided to go in that night because we had received a report that Darja, one of the underage girls whom we had helped rescue from a brothel five months earlier, had been resold by her mother and sister and was being used as a prostitute again. It is our practice not to advise the police in advance of an investigation in a red-light area of our intentions. This is because of the high level of corruption and tip-offs that can occur, resulting in a higher component of risk in an investigation such as this. On this particular evening, we were expecting a routine investigation as Pranit and the two other investigators searched the area for Darja and any other minor girls forced to sell themselves.

Then the cell phone rang. It was Pranit shouting, "Help me! A mob is forming around me. They're beating me!"

My colleague and I yelled, "Go, go, go!" and Rajiv gunned the Indian-made Tata Sumo SUV as we headed into the red-light district.

We didn't have to go far before we saw a knot of people in the street with Pranit at the center. Later, we would learn that a brothel owner, a woman named Kamala Bai, apparently recognized that Pranit had been with us at the restaurant a few days earlier and knew that we were continuing our investigation of the sex trade in the area. Pranit had a covert camera on him, and the images later showed the fat brothel owner coming up to him on the street, grabbing him, and demanding that he say what he was doing there. When he didn't give satisfactory answers, a collection of pimps, brothel keepers, thugs, and others who made their living off the flesh trade quickly gathered around. Fortunately, the growing mob, while roughing him up and pulling at him, never discovered his undercover camera, with the lens hidden in his shirt pocket. Had they discovered it, who knows what would have occurred?

At the same time, our two other investigators, who had infiltrated the Gokul Nagar lanes lined with brothels, had their own covert cameras running. When we reviewed the film later, it was haunting to see the young thugs running by the dozens down the alleys to join the fray when they heard that a mob was forming. Back where Pranit was, some of the young men began punching him and the women began throwing chili pepper in his face. The number in the mob at the time we arrived exceeded one hundred.

And then things got worse.

As we drove up, my colleague jumped out of the car and tried to pull Pranit inside. Some in the crowd evidently recognized him as one who had taken part in the May 20 raid in Gokul Nagar, and they quickly grew even more enraged. The mob now had grown to more than three hundred. Several of them pushed Pranit to the ground and began hitting and kicking him. In the meantime, more people in the mob were throwing chili powder, while others scratched, hit, and pulled in the mob.

Despite the abuse he was taking, my colleague didn't fight back. Instead, he managed to grab hold of Pranit from the ground, and between the two of us, we succeeded in getting the three of us back into the car and pulled the door closed. We locked the doors and believed that we were safe for the moment.

That's when I looked forward and realized that our driver, Rajiv, in the midst of the fight, had fled the car. I leaned forward from the back seat into the front seat to start the engine in his absence and realized that, when Rajiv left the car, he took the keys with him. (We found out later that he had decided to go for the police, but all we knew at the time was that Rajiv was gone!) We were stuck there, unable to drive away, with the seething crowd all around us. We had no idea what would come next.

By this time, the excited mob of people outside our vehicle were gesturing at us and yelling, with their faces up against the windows. Then some of the men in the crowd decided that they would hurl rocks at the car, which had briefly been our refuge. The first rock bounced off the windshield of the Tata Sumo. The second rock broke through a side window. Most of the rest of the windows soon collapsed in a sea of shattered glass as the brothel owners and their supporters continued their assault on our SUV with different-sized rocks. I recall wondering where all of the rocks were coming from!

Two large rocks the size of melons were thrown into the vehicle while we sat inside. One of them hit my arm, drawing blood, while another hit Pranit. Thankfully, the violence abated as the crowd saw that we were waiting quietly inside the car. People still shouted at us occasionally, and the odd fist came through the glassless windows, but none of them found their target and the acts of violence subsided. We stayed put and so did the crowd.

More than half an hour passed before a lone policeman rode on his motorcycle into Gokul Nagar, where we sat in the shell of our windowless SUV. I was amazed to see that the policeman had as his only weapon a wooden stick. I was also a little amused that the passenger on the back of the motorcycle was one of our investigators, who had made his way to the police station to report the mob attack on us. When the lone policeman arrived, the remaining crowd scattered. It was obvious that the people were terrified of the police. The officers escorted us as we drove our disheveled, windowless SUV out of the red-light area. We were taken to the police station for questioning.

I soon learned that the reason that the police are so feared is their well-earned reputation for ruthlessly beating those whom they question in order to get answers. Fortunately, we were dealt with quite differently because we were Americans.

Our first objective was to make sure that the undercover footage we had of the investigation and attack was made secure. We quickly handed off the covert cameras, recorders, and tapes so that they remained with our colleagues. Had the police known of this evidence, we didn't know how it would be dealt with and we were through taking chances for the night.

The police station consisted of two main rooms. The first was the office of the chief of police and the other was the interrogation room. In the interrogation room was a two-foot-long belt with a wooden handle. It was obvious that this is what was used to extract information from those they questioned, and it was left in plain view for those entering the room. It was well worn. After a short time, two officers came in to write down our statements of what had occurred. In the West, the process of having a statement taken is just that—they write down what you say. Not so in Sangli, India. It seemed to be more of a consensus-building exercise, and what we had to say seemed to be of only nominal interest as the officers decided what our statements were to consist of. We were glad that the videotape record was secure. We were then taken to the hospital to get cleaned up.

At the hospital, the brothel owners sent one of their thugs to try to intimidate us. He sat on bench next to us and spoke loudly. His breath was sour and smelled of a hard night of drinking. We were in no mood to put up with anything more from the brothel owners that night and let him know it plainly. Any veiled threats were also dwarfed by the intensity of the scene in the hospital. Government hospitals in India are filthy, unsanitary places. The metal shelves are virtually bare of any medical supplies, and one lone syringe was on the medical table. I had no intention of having that put into my arm for any reason!

Evidence of the harsh and cruel unwritten rules that apply to low-caste females became apparent when a woman was wheeled into my room and the rusty gurney she was lying on came to a squeaky stop next to me. She struggled for a few minutes, gasped for breath, then died. No attention was given to her. It was as if her life had ended perhaps as it had begun—a non-event. An old rag was put over her head after she passed. She wasn't treated; she wasn't even wheeled away. She had simply been discarded.

Meanwhile, we learned later that the police took several of our attackers to the Vishrambag police station in Sangli for closer questioning, since our driver, Rajiv, had lodged a formal complaint. I was aware that frightful things can happen inside the "interrogation room" of Vishrambag, and so I didn't envy the brothel keepers and thugs going in there, despicable as their work is. Given the close relationship between the prostitution bosses and the Sangli police, I'm not surprised that in the end no one was arrested for the attack on us and our vehicle.

Now, you might think that while I was sitting inside that SUV I would have been wondering what I—a middle-aged American lawyer—was doing in one of the worst neighborhoods in South Asia with my arm bleeding and an angry mob surging around me. Truthfully, what I felt then was a pervading sense of peace in my spirit. I won't say that I didn't send up some quick prayers for our safety, but whatever the outcome would be, I was at peace knowing that I was where I should be, doing what I should be doing: helping to locate and rescue girls like Darja and Karishma who are forced into prostitution—and keeping them out of the sex racket for good.

My teammates and I received injuries at the hands of a mob in Sangli, India.

Joining the Fray

In the twenty-first-century war between slavery and liberation, the combatants on the wrong side are legion. Among these are organized crime bosses and their thugs, unscrupulous business owners, crooked politicians and corrupt law enforcement officers, relatives who put money ahead of children, abductors of persons, transnational shippers of persons, retailers who don't care where their goods come from, and rapists with money in their pockets. These take advantage of poverty, ignorance, greed, social disruption, selfishness, violence, discrimination, perversion, and other evils for the sake of the money they get out of participating in the enslavement of others. And given that the history of slavery is as old as the annals of human

Our Commitment

Restore International condemns trafficking in persons and is committed to fighting this scourge and protecting victims who fall prey to traffickers. Our commitment to eradicate trafficking includes:

• seeking a more vigorous enforcement of existing laws against those who traffic in persons

• maximizing media coverage to raise awareness about human trafficking and how it can be eradicated

• conducting investigations to identify, protect, and rescue children exploited by traffickers

• encouraging the UN and other NGOs to work with Restore to combat this crime and hold traffickers accountable through effective prosecution

This work is vital to the sustainable future of nations around the world and to the eradication of deplorable acts such as trafficking in children.

civilization, it might seem that these people are inevitably on the winning side of the war. But, then again, arrayed against them are some potent forces.

International organizations, such as the United Nations itself, along with subgroups such as the International Labor Organization, help to set standards for human rights, monitor international trafficking, and to some extent coordinate efforts to end the global slave trade. Most national governments have passed laws and are making efforts to interdict human trafficking within their own spheres of control, with the U.S. State Department's Office to Monitor and Combat Trafficking in Persons notably taking the lead among the nation-states. Certain individuals—government, business, or religious leaders, along with celebrities as diverse as Latin singer Ricky Martin and Sweden's Queen Silvia—lend their clout and expertise to anti-trafficking efforts. And then there is the vast assortment of nongovernmental organizations (NGOs for short), secular and faith-based, small and large, narrowly focused and widely targeted, that enable like-minded people to band together in opposing enslavement—familiar names like Amnesty International, Human Rights Watch, and the International Justice Mission come to mind. It may be that even this impressive aggregate of forces will never be able to eradicate human slavery entirely, so long as wickedness lurks in the human heart. It is because of their efforts that slavery is no worse than it already is, and it is because of them that we can hope that one day slavery might become a negligible factor among the violations of human rights in the world.

Let's remember that there are likely at least 27 million enslaved people in the world today. The battle is far from over, and there is more than enough room on the field for more people to get involved on the right side of trying to put an end to human slavery. In short, there's room for you. You don't need to be an international organization; you don't need to be wealthy; you don't need to advertise what you do to others; you don't need to identify what you do as a denominational or religious activity. Most of all, you don't need to wait and think about it some more. What you need to do is show up. Likewise, when I first encountered modern-day slavery during a trip to India in 2002, I decided that I would be one of the ones who would try to contribute whatever energy or creativity I had to try to save some of the victims.[1] Then I was wise enough to surround myself with people who were more creative and energetic than me. Now, together, we feel like we have more to contribute than we could individually.

Given that by some estimates *more than half* of the world's slaves live in India,[2] I reasonably thought this was a good place to get started. The human tragedy which has unfolded in Uganda, with over twenty years of civil war and millions victimized, is the next door through which we seemed to be drawn. Since the forms of slavery and injustice that seemed to me most heinous and most inexcusable—the kind that pained my heart the greatest—was forced child prostitution and abuse of children and the poor overseas, I chose to assemble a team to start making a difference right now. I decided to form my own NGO to help get it done, and in 2004 Restore International was born and started its work in India.

au•da•cious
adjective [3]

1 a : intrepidly daring : ADVENTUROUS *an audacious mountain climber* b : recklessly bold : RASH *an audacious maneuver*

2 : contemptuous of religion, or decorum : INSOLENT

3 : marked by originality and verve *audacious experiments*

MAP OF INDIA

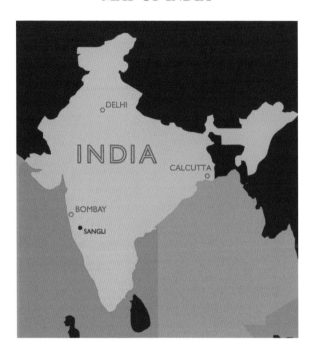

[showing location where RI works]

Restore International

Everyone at Restore International shares a common strand of DNA in our approach to these serious and sad problems. We love the definition of an "audacious" approach to the problems we are trying to tackle. Isn't this just a great way to define an approach that integrates faith, conviction, and a desire to serve those in desperate need?

While each of us on the team is far from manifesting all of these wonderful characteristics, when I look around the table at who we have working both domestically and overseas, I see us living into most of the attributes that make for an audacious outfit. And that's what we want to be. Restore International attempts to find audacious ways to restore justice to children and the poorest of the poor. As a result, we hope to participate in those things that will restore freedom, restore dignity, and restore hope. This is what Restore International is seeking to do for victims of enslavement.

We began our work in the South Indian states of Maharashtra, Karnataka, Andhra Pradesh, and Tamil Nadu. We chose not to focus on the largest cities, such as Mumbai (Bombay), where other groups have already begun working to reduce the traffic in underage prostitutes. Instead, we decided to work in the smaller cities, such as the city of Miraj where Karishma was working, because there the illegal flesh trade had largely been overlooked. Many of these cities are located at the crossroads of highways and are visited regularly by commercial truckers, who make up a large percentage of the customers at Indian brothels. (These truckers little realize that a part of the freight they are transporting across India is HIV/AIDS.) In many of these out-of-the-way places, prostitution both legal and illegal is permitted to flourish, and many of the red-light districts are as large as those in much bigger cities.

I am privileged to lead many outstanding human rights workers at Restore International. All of the people involved with our organization are fearless and tireless crusaders for the liberation of young girls in the most dire of circumstances. Even more, they are the kind of people that you would want to hang out with. They are just plain good people.

The young Indian attorney who worked with us in all of the interventions discussed in this book brought his considerable expertise in Indian law and custom to help us defeat child prostitution in the courts of his nation. In addition to this man, our ranks have included investigators who go into the brothels to uncover the illegal activity, and caseworkers who ensure that the rescued girls don't slip through the cracks of the social system in India or elsewhere. Every one of us is passionate about the work of saving the Karishmas of India and other countries.

I am thankful for anyone who, for whatever reason, is seeking to end human slavery or to care

Roles within Restore International

Neither Restore International nor any other NGO in the country could be as effective without the dedicated service of people with specialized skills in well-defined roles in our efforts overseas.

• An *advocate* interacts with public and private leaders on the subject of child prostitution as well as follows up on the prosecution of perpetrators and the aftercare of victims.

• An *investigator* locates minor girls in prostitution, performs undercover surveillance, and supports rescue operations.

• An *administrator* runs the daily operations of the office, managing performance plans and expenditures.

• A *counselor* ensures that rescued girls are getting the care they are entitled to and conducts group psychotherapy.

• A *social worker* participates in rescues and tracks rescued girls on a casework basis.

• An *accountant* is responsible for financial records, reporting, and taxes.

for its victims. And, whenever it seems useful, I will gladly partner with any group or individual to accomplish the tasks our organization has set out to achieve. Certainly I've met many people of goodwill in India—judges, lawyers, police officers, government officials, NGO workers, and others— whose hearts are broken like mine over the plight of India's kids forced into prostitution. But, for me, and for those who work with me at Restore International, our motivation is more than just a humanitarian impulse. We are people of faith who are responding to Jesus's call to love our neighbor as ourselves and, like the good Samaritan, to go out of our way to help those who are different from us and yet who are suffering and in need.[4]

Restore International is not an evangelistic organization. Indeed, India's Foreigners Act (1946) puts restrictions on how visitors to the country may engage in religious preaching, its Foreign Contribution Regulation Act limits how outside money can be spent on religious purposes, and several Indian states at certain times have had anti-conversion laws on the books.[5] While we regret the limitations placed on religious freedom in India, we nevertheless comply with the legal restrictions on proselytism and focus on rescuing and caring for underage prostitutes who have been illegally detained. We cooperate with other groups without getting hung up on what label they may have, be it Protestant, Roman Catholic, or others. Again, the only distinction that we saw Jesus making had nothing to do with sect and denomination. He made it clear that the special spot in God's heart was carved out for kids and the poor. And so we hope that in its own way our work offers a silent witness to the love of God for these two groups.

In time, the scope of Restore International's work will broaden— probably broaden a great deal (see chapter ten). Not only do we expect to begin working in other parts of India soon, but also we plan to continue to spread our activities to other nations around the world. We have already moved beyond solely rescuing kids from brothels and started advocating on behalf of bonded laborers, child soldiers, internally displaced persons, victims of war, and other persons trapped in a range of coerced working and living conditions. Every form of slavery is an affront to God-given human dignity, and it is our intention to help remove this black mark from face of the world.

Our activities fall into a four-part strategy.

A Strategy to Restore Life

A piecemeal approach will never bring the child prostitution system in the world to its knees. A fly-by-night presence will never make a lasting change in the lives of victimized girls. Only a comprehensive plan, applied doggedly, will make a real difference for the young girls tricked or coerced into the sex trade. And that's why at Restore International we have developed the four-part strategy of investigation, intervention, legal action, and aftercare that is equally applicable in any country where we operate.

1. Investigation. To rescue girls trapped in prostitution, we first must find them, and so we seek information in as many ways as possible. Often we send in an undercover investigator posing as a brothel customer, as we did with Pranit Mayakunar on the night when we were attacked by a mob in Sangli. But, brothel keepers are sometimes careful to keep their youngest prostitutes out of public sight. So then we must rely on information given by various people. These informants may be rescued girls who know of other girls in the same plight as they were in, or they may be police officers, NGO workers, or others who have knowledge about a particular red-light district.

2. Intervention. Since in too many cases the local police are lackadaisical about enforcing anti-child prostitution laws, if not actually complicit in the crime, we have to push them to go in and arrest the perpetrators and release the victims. When we are successful at persuading them, we will go along with them to show them where the girls are (and to make sure the police do their job). We ensure that the police separate the girls from the brothel keepers and send the girls to a government home where they can receive initial care.

3. Legal action. Courts are often slow and not always effective. We try to ensure that a rescued girl is remanded before the court and sent to a medical professional for age verification. We protect her from unscrupulous lawyers who might try to help the brothel keepers regain custody of her. We encourage police to close the brothel where the crime was committed. Also, we oppose bail for the criminals, organize witnesses and testimony for the prosecutors, and, if necessary, appeal an acquittal.

4. Aftercare. The suffering that brothel girls undergo does great physical and psychological harm, and their release raises questions about what they are going to do next. In many cases they are uneducated and can't return home, because it was their families who sold them in the first place. Meanwhile, the brothel keepers might be after them to try to get them back.

So, following their release, we make sure that the girls go into the safe custody of a government-run rehabilitation institution. Where we can, we also offer them education, job training, counseling, and access to medical care.

Our goal in this process is to make a permanent change in a terrible situation. We want to make it impossible for a pedophile to find a child to satisfy his perversion in the cities where we operate. We want to put the slaveholders of these girls in prison for a good long time. And we want to help restore the victimized girls to as much health of spirit, mind, and body as we can. Common humanity and our faith demand no less of us.

In the chapters that follow, we will look at each piece of Restore International's strategy more closely. First up: the investigations—how we find minor girls imprisoned in India's brothels and put together enough information to get them out.

SIX

Brothel Detectives

Restore International Strategy Part 1—Investigation

The reason that Restore International investigator Pranit Mayakunar, our operations chief, and I were attacked by a mob in the Gokul Nagar red-light district of Sangli, India (a story told in the previous chapter), was because the brothel bosses there had been put on alert by a rescue of underage prostitutes we had initiated some months earlier. Our team had helped to free seventeen young girls from their sex bondage in Gokul Nagar. The story began even earlier than that, however, as our investigators infiltrated the brothel district over a period of several days to verify the presence of minor girls being prostituted in violation of Indian law.

Gokul Nagar is much like the red-light district where Karishma was being prostituted in nearby Miraj, except that it is even larger.[g] Occupying an area about half a mile square, Gokul Nagar has a main street down the center of it, with four cross streets, each made of dirt and about ten feet wide. The brothels are narrow, dirty houses—little more than stalls filled with wooden partitions separating lines of rusty metal beds—and are packed closely together along with shabby shops and homes. Prostitutes sit or stand beside the doors of their brothels, with pimps and keepers watching over them from nearby. Men of all ages troll the streets in search of a girl or woman who appeals to them.

There is no question about who the real sheriffs are in what has the feel of a Wild West town within a city. In fact, a sign prominently displayed at the entrance to Gokul Nagar lists the names of the brothel owners for all to see. It is, in effect, a warning sign to others about where the real power and influence are. And it was well settled that no one would dare to cross the line with the brothel owners, because it meant crossing swords with them. So even though it was well known that little girls were peddled by these traffickers of flesh, no one dared to disrupt the brothel owners' unfettered power. Not even the police. It simply never occurred. Ever.

During the team's first visit to Sangli, Pranit and Jahab, our investigators, found the flesh trade revolting, but they put aside their personal reaction to Gokul Nagar and relied on their acting ability to pretend to be two more of the many customers walking up and down the streets, checking out the "merchandise." Indeed, they looked little different from the other Indian men in the neighborhood. But, what the others around them did not know was that under their shirts they had tiny surveillance cameras that they would surreptitiously turn on to record illegal activity.

Pranit and Jahab used several typical techniques to get information about young girls in the brothels. For one thing, just walking up and down the streets gave them a chance to look at many of the prostitutes on duty and identify a few girls who appeared to be under the age of eighteen. They also talked to pimps and brothel owners and said they were interested in very young girls who might be concealed inside the brothels. When the pimps or brothel owners said that they had this type of merchandise, one of the investigators would go into a brothel, give money to the madam, and go into a room with the girl and merely sit with her, asking her about her name and age and where she came from—all caught on tape. At the end of a few forays into Gokul Nagar, Pranit and Jahab had located several girls whom they felt confident were underage.

Our team took this information to the district superintendent of police, Milind Bharambe, in Sangli. Surprisingly, the superintendent seemed more open than some Indian police would be to staging a raid on the red-light district. In fact, he explained that he didn't want to send in officers if they might net only one or a few minor girls; he wanted to get all of them! If our people could bring him information on all the brothels of Gokul Nagar, then Bharambe would listen and consider a wide-reaching and first-ever raid of the area. If not, then there would be no raid at all.

At this point our people took a gamble. Not wanting to lose the opportunity of sparking a rescue, our country director took the bold and brave step of going into Gokul Nagar himself to gather information. (A white man is rather conspicuous.) He went to every brothel he could find, and when he came upon one, he would go up to the brothel owner, offer a small gift of chocolates or even contraceptives, and say that he was from an NGO and was conducting a survey of the area. Then he would ask the owner specific questions, such as "What is your name? How many girls do you have here? What are their ages?" While asking his questions and noting down the responses, he made sure to act as friendly as he could—little did the brothel owners know that this was a precursor to a raid! Since the brothel owners had been allowed to conduct their business unhindered for a long time, they had little suspicion and were remarkably forthcoming with information about the inmates of their houses of prostitution. This cavalier attitude regarding grossly illegal and morally corrupt conduct struck me as evidence that such ultimate power that the brothel owners had not only destroys the innocent, but also deludes the powerful.

Now we had maps of the brothel locations, the names of brothel owners, and a clearer idea of where the minor girls were. Our people took all of the information to Milind Bharambe, and the superintendent was at last satisfied and began laying plans for one of the largest brothel raids by police in that part of India. It would also be one of Restore International's most successful operations to date.

When a John Is Not a John

Our country director, Pranit, and Jahab were carrying out the crucial first part of the Restore International strategy: they were investigating the extent of wrongdoing in a brothel area and the existence of minor girls.

Restore International fields small groups of trained men and women in various countries who can be deployed to areas where we believe children are being forced to sexually serve others. The investigative team's goal is to accumulate enough evidence to justify a police intervention in a brothel area, leading to the arrest of perpetrators and the rescue of girls involved in forced prostitution. Their work serves as the foundation for everything else we do to help these girls.

Our team members working in the field locate suitable men and women to serve as investigators and participate in in-the-field training. Some of these people have prior experience in human rights work; all of them have the skills and the temperament for doing this important work. They are bold and yet patient in uncovering information about victims of sex trafficking. They are willing to risk their own well-being, and possibly even their lives, in order to seek justice for girls who are living in some of the worst conditions imaginable.

Sometimes the investigators come up with the needed evidence to release prostituted girls through the network of informants they painstakingly develop. These informants can include sympathetic police officers, members of local nongovernmental or community-based organizations, and other individuals with knowledge of what is going on in red-light districts. Interviews with previously rescued victims can also turn up leads about other young girls who are still being held in sexual captivity, and thus one intervention can often lead to another and another.

Beyond the intelligence provided by informants, our operatives gather evidence through their own direct investigations in the field. That is, they go into places where underage prostitutes might be working and gather information that can be used to prove wrongdoing.

There are various ways that young girls can be located, and many of the groups involved in this type of work adopt one or more. One strategy is to stage a sting operation. Under this approach, investigators might rent a room at one of the "lodges" (motels) that are known for providing prostitutes to their customers. The investigator then simply says to the proprietor of the lodge, "I'd like you to get me a young girl." Shortly afterward, a car arrives with several girls of around twelve to fourteen years of age in it, and the investigator chooses one, pays the pimp, and takes the girl up to his room, where on tape he questions her about her name, age, and so on. If all goes well, the sting operation can uncover enough information to shut down not only the brothel from which the girl came, but also the lodge where she and other young girls are taken to be abused.

While a lodge sting can be remarkably effective for those trying to rescue minor girls, more often our investigators go to the primary source of the child prostitution problem: the brothel area itself. Brothels can be densely located in one area of the city or they can be scattered along a section of a major highway and consist of small, crudely furnished houses, abandoned buses, and even dilapidated shacks.

On a particularly dark evening, made even more ominous by rapid flashes of lightning and raps of thunder, we made our way along an abandoned stretch of highway where India's mass of gravel and freight trucks crisscrossed the country. Every quarter of a mile, a small flickering kerosene lamp could be found that indicated the presence of a roadside brothel. I watched as every five to ten minutes, the drivers of a truck full of freight would pull over to inspect the women for sale and decide whether to punctuate the dull all-night drive with a stop at the brothel. The spread of HIV/AIDS in India is fueled by this commonplace highway scene.

Whether in a city or roadside brothel, the way it usually works (as in the case of Pranit and Jahab in Sangli) is that a pair of investigators will go into a red-light district posing as customers. In India, male friends frequently travel in pairs and go into these areas together, so it surprises no one that our investigators are there together. In this case, though, the two are not out for a night of carousing; they are working in tandem to keep each other safe. Meanwhile, exit routes have been carefully mapped out in advance and other team members are positioned where appropriate in an automobile a short distance away, ready to come for the investigators if they call and say they are in trouble.

Typically, the investigators start by trolling the streets of the red-light district by foot or in a hired motor rickshaw. They are looking for minor prostitutes who are standing around and waiting for a customer. They can also engage one of the many pimps of the area in conversation and ask him where they can find a young girl. Sadly, this is not an unusual request. If the pimp is unsuspecting about the investigators' true motive, he will conduct one of them to a brothel where our team member can find what he is looking for.

Once in the brothel, the investigator negotiates the transaction (in that culture, he has to haggle or else someone would get suspicious) and finally gets alone with the girl. At that point, he quickly tells the girl something like "I guess I'm not in the mood tonight, after all. Can we just talk?" And then he proceeds to try to put her at her ease and get her to open up. He wants to find out such facts as who she is, where she is from, how old she is, how long she has been working there, what the name of her brothel keeper is, how much money she earns and how much of it she gets to keep, how she is treated, whether the local police know about her presence in the brothel, and so forth.

All of this goes onto videotape, as our investigators are equipped with advanced surveillance equipment. The camera itself is taped to their back or concealed in a fanny pack, and a cable runs under the investigator's shirt to his shirt pocket, where a lens is concealed in a pager or shirt pocket button. Through a pinhole opening, the camera records the conversation with the pimp, the transaction with the brothel keeper, and the interview with the young victim.

Brothel customers normally spend only a short period of time with the prostitutes, and so, if he is not to arouse suspicion by staying too long, the investigator posing as a customer may not be able to get all the information he needs in just one visit. In that case he might say to the girl before he leaves, "Is it okay if I come back? I like you and I want to see you again." Then he'll try to complete his investigation later. If all goes well—that is, if the girl is forthcoming about her story and no one gets suspicious—a case can be made to the police that they ought to come in and pull this girl out of her captivity.

Make no mistake: there are lots of unknown variables when carrying out an investigation in a place like Gokul Nagar, and things can go very wrong very quickly.

One of our investigators was conducting an investigation in the red-light district of Pune when he detected a very young girl being offered to customers. After making inquiries about her, he was conducted to a brothel. Inside, our investigator was immediately surrounded by several *hijras*, or eunuchs, who were acting as the girl's brothel keepers. India's eunuchs are often large and mean, and perhaps because of his accent or demeanor, they suspected that our investigator was not a real customer. Consequently they forced him to take off his shirt so that they could look for concealed equipment on him. Fortunately, on this occasion, he wasn't wearing a camera, since he was doing initial reconnaissance and had not expected to go into a brothel. Our investigator got out without harm, but the eunuchs' threats made it a terrifying experience for him.

I, myself, on one occasion experienced what it was like to be at risk as an investigator. One late night in 2005, this same investigator and were I walking through a red-light area in Kolhapur when we decided to go a hundred yards up a dark labyrinth of unlit lanes. We were looking for little girls forced to prostitute themselves. All seemed to be going well at first, but then my companion, who speaks Tamil, overheard one man in the street saying to another about me in that language, "Hey, that guy's got a camera on him." I don't know how they could tell I was wearing a camera, but they figured it out.

We exchanged a couple of quick whispers to put a game plan together for getting out, but before we could react, a crowd quickly began to form, as happened during the mob attack in Sangli. The backup members of our team, sitting in an SUV a quarter of a mile away, had no idea what was occurring. I recall feeling a bit like Dorothy in *The Wizard of Oz* and like I was a long way from Kansas at that time. More effective than just clicking our heels and wishing we were elsewhere, we just plain found our way out of there in a hurry. By God's grace, it was another narrow escape.

The most common danger is not that someone will notice a camera (it was a fluke with me in Kolhapur), but that someone will notice that an investigator is not a local. Despite the unknowns, our investigators have been tremendously successful at what they do. Their skill and training take them through the obstacle course of risks, and in the end, by God's providence, they get the information they need. Little do the trafficked girls held in the brothels know it, but among them walk men willing to take risks so that they can know a life of freedom and hope.

Preparing for a Rescue

Once an investigative team feels that it has adequate information to request a raid of the brothels by the police, there are several steps they still have to take in order to get ready for a successful rescue. The first is to compile the information in a well-documented form.

India's Code of Criminal Procedure provides a format for evidence,[2] and investigators generally seek to follow that format. This involves compiling such materials as statements from eyewitnesses and photographic evidence of underage girls involved in prostitution transactions. Sometimes, however, it is more advantageous to conceal certain facts from the police at this initial stage. For example, team members may be concerned that corrupt police officers will tip off brothel owners if they know that we are interested in the activities of certain brothels. And so, in such cases, investigators may put together a simple letter stating that they have reason to believe that laws are being broken in a brothel district.

Investigator Profile: Mohal

Mohal is affectionately known by myself and everyone else on our team as "Mighty Mohal" because he is fearless in the pursuit of justice. He has been threatened and beaten up more than once, but he is still filled with eagerness to help modern-day slaves and others who are socially marginalized or who have no voice in their society.

I met Mohal when he served as an interpreter for me on one of my first trips to India. He is in his mid-twenties, comes from a poor family, and lives with his grandparents. We took an immediate liking to each other, and we decided that we would work to change the nation of India and serve the poor together. He not only participates in the investigations and interventions we carry out in India's brothels, but also heads up our Snethikar operations, putting former bonded laborers and other disadvantaged people to work. (For more on Snethikar, see chapter ten.)

Years ago, Mohal would address me only as "sir" in every conversation, no matter how informal. As we have become the best of friends over the years, he still refuses to refer to me as "Bob," thinking it too informal

(cont'd on next page)

(and he also thinks it's a funny-sounding name), so he simply calls me "Goff." No exceptions.

A little-known fact about Mohal is that ever since he was orphaned as a child, he had wanted a drum set. In the village where he is from, such things are not commonplace, so at the end of one trip with my family (including extended family member and musician Brandon Heath), we found a musical instrument store in Chennai and surprised Mohal and sent him back with perhaps the biggest and shiniest fire-engine-red drum set and cymbals I've ever seen. For weeks after our return to the United States, our home phone would ring in the middle of the night (daytime in India), and when I would answer in a groggy voice, there would be no words spoken, only the crashing of cymbals, the banging of tom-tom drums, and the thunder of a hundred rapid beats of the snare. Then the phone would simply click off.

Mohal is pure joy to Team Goff, and we love him like a son.

Whatever form the written report may take, staff members hand-deliver it to a senior officer in the local police department and request that the police initiate action under section 15 of the Immoral Trafficking (Prevention) Act.[3] At the same time, they offer to provide vehicles (which the police are sometimes without) as well as personnel who will go along with the police on the rescue operation, show them the location of the brothel(s) in question, and provide bogus customers who can get evidence of illegal prostitution on the night of the rescue by arranging to hire the services of an underage girl. They also offer to provide *panchas* (witnesses), at least one of whom will be a female social worker who will observe the search and assist the police in taking charge of the girls. Finally, they offer an Indian citizen to be the complainant in the case, officially initiating the legal response to the raid by filling out a First Information Report following the rescue operation.[4]

Sometimes the police readily agree to carry out a rescue operation, coordinating fully with the human rights staff. Other times, though, they are more reluctant, since they may think they have more important things to do or because they are themselves involved in the sex trade by taking bribes from brothel owners and by using the prostitutes as customers. But, the team members don't take no for an answer. They keep asking again and again, if necessary going over the local police officer's head to a district superintendent who is more sympathetic to our cause. The bottom line is, they do what they have to do to persuade the police to go in. And once they get agreement from the police to do a rescue, they attempt to get an acknowledgment from them in writing about when and where they will carry out the operation.

With a rescue date and time scheduled, the personnel who are going to be involved in the operation meet for a briefing session. They go over each step of the plan and make sure that everyone fully understands his or her role in the intervention. If they have maps or photos of the brothels to be targeted, they circulate those so that everyone knows exactly where they are headed. They designate who will be the rescue leader and assign roles of bogus customers, complainant, and *panch* witnesses.

At this point, the initial investigation comes to an end and the intervention begins, but that is not the end of the investigators' work.

Staying on the Case

After a rescue operation has taken place, there are still a number of follow-up operations that require the skills of a trained investigator. For example, if brothel keepers dispute the medical age verification of rescued girls, claiming that these girls are really eighteen or older (this is often the case), investigators will track down birth certificates and school documents to prove that the girls are minors.

And after a police raid has been carried out in a certain red-light district, investigators will return some time later to check and make sure that there are no more underage girls being exploited there. We want interventions to stick. Because the brothel owners are keenly aware of who is in their cities, the investigators merely being back in the city can have a huge deterrent effect.

The most common kind of follow-up investigation after a police raid is keeping track of the rescued girls. Investigators seek to ensure that the girls are being properly taken care of and

Mobile Investigation Units

The investigative, intervention, and prosecution activities of Restore International initially have been based upon the concept of conducting strategic interventions through the deployment of mobile intervention units (MIUs). With the exception of a few large red-light areas in Calcutta, Mumbai, and Delhi, places of prostitution in India are generally located in slumlike neighborhoods that consist of densely populated communities where news travels fast and law enforcement action creates a powerful impact. Therefore, interventions initiated by Restore International have been capable of creating a deterrent effect quickly and substantially reducing the occurrence of child prostitution. This allows an MIU to move on to another city or region within a relatively short period of time.

As our strategy was developed, it was contemplated that a MIU would be comprised of up to ten people serving as investigators, lawyers, and social workers. According to the plan, each MIU would be divided into two teams. Team A would focus on carrying out investigations to identify minor girls in prostitution,

(cont'd on next page)

conveying that information to the police, and conducting an intervention to rescue those girls. Team B would be deployed just before Team A leaves the target location to focus on follow-up in court, aftercare tasks, and home inquiry trips to the villages of the rescued girls. Each member of the MIU planned to be in the field at least ten days per month. One difficulty that we have confronted has been keeping pace with this agreed-upon schedule. The toll has been significant as a result of our unwavering insistence that we *do*, not merely *consider* or *plan* for later. For the little girls held in bondage, there is no "later," and they are little interested in our plans and excuses for not acting now.

In the plan, a strategic intervention begins when an MIU deploys to a targeted city, finds minor girls through investigation, and initiates a raid. Once the raid is complete, social workers begin to counsel the girls, network with other NGOs to find vacancies for the girls in aftercare facilities, and engage in home inquiries. The advocates ensure placement of the girls in safe custody, oppose bail applications for the perpetrators, and coordinate

(cont'd on next page)

that they are available to serve as witnesses once the case comes to trial. The problem is that, in India, the gap of time between the arrest of brothel keepers and their trial can be many months or even years. That's more than enough time for the rescued girls to move on to a new life and drop out of our sight. Somehow, in the populous and disorderly nation of India, it is easy for people to disappear. We don't want that to occur with the rescued girls.

The tracking process starts almost immediately after the rescue. Investigators offer their services to help government social workers conduct the required home studies once girls have been rescued. In other words, while a former prostitute is housed in a government facility, a social worker is supposed to go to the village where a particular girl came from and interview her family to determine whether it is safe to release her back into their custody. (Since they may be the ones who sold her in the first place, this is often not a good idea.) The social workers are not always diligent in conducting these home studies, so investigators try to go with them to verify home addresses and ensure that the social worker has a true picture of what the girl would be getting into if she were returned home.

Returning to her village is only one of the options for a rescued girl. The fact is, after being released from brothel captivity, the girls scatter. Some may be pulled back into prostitution despite all our efforts and those of the government social workers to prevent it. Others go into long-term care at a private aftercare facility, until they reach the age of eighteen. Others drift to different places in India and may get married or take a job and live on their own.

Wherever a girl goes, investigators periodically follow up to keep track of her whereabouts. If she has been retrafficked, then they try to rescue her again. If she is living a life of freedom, they check to see if she needs anything and keep encouraging her to take part in the trial once it comes. She most likely would prefer to put her past behind her, yet her testimony can be crucial in putting perpetrators in jail where they will be unable to victimize other children. As a trial comes near, human rights workers give the information about the girl to the prosecutor, who can prepare her for giving her testimony.

To give an idea of what it is like doing follow-up investigations involving prostitution slavery in India, let me tell you about my trip to a remote village to find one of the victims.

information gathering from the rescued girls. Efforts are made to ensure accurate age verification tests.

As planned, Team A and Team B are intended to overlap on site so that there will be a continuous Restore International presence in the targeted city until the entire strategic intervention is complete. This occurs when the rescued girls are placed in safe custody and the initial bail applications of the accused are disposed of in court. Each strategic intervention in the MIU model should take approximately twenty days.

When our investigative team arrived at the village of a girl who had been retrafficked, we were greeted by men with weapons, as they knew there would be consequences.

Days in the Life of an Investigator

The rescue operation in Gokul Nagar, like other rescues, generated a need for further information gathering and follow-up investigations. So in October some Restore International investigators and I arrived in Sangli to continue building a case for protection of minor girls and prosecution for their exploiters. Like peeling an onion, we find that when we perform rescues and insist that India's laws be enforced, we find any number of sources that contribute to the circumstance where young girls are abused. Our interventions somehow kick off a whole series of oppositions to our attempts to expose the truth. Indeed, what we discovered after raiding Gokul Nagar was that, when commerce is being affected, the stakes grow exponentially higher. It has been like that throughout history—those who have and abuse power will fight to maintain it.

The day we arrived in Sangli, we went to the courthouse to locate records we needed to continue prosecuting the perpetrators. We then made attempts to meet with the district collector to advance our petition that the brothels run by the arrested owners be shut down. Our position was that, after the May raid, the court had ordered that the brothels not return to Gokul Nagar to transact business. The information we had collected from our follow-up investigations indicated that these owners went directly back into the red-light area in violation of the court's express order. Needless to say, all of this was more than enough activity to gain notice for us—news of our arrival in Sangli spread quickly, and the other side started to respond.

By the second evening we spent in the area, some of the brothel owners had tracked us to the hotel where we were staying to pay us a visit. Ironically, at the time that we were they were at our hotel looking for us, we were in their brothels in the red-light area looking for them. When we returned to the hotel late that night, we learned from the front desk manager that we had received a group of unhappy visitors. We were a bit worried that they might find out which rooms we were staying in and visit us again in the middle of the night. (These people were capable of violence.) Since we were too tired to move to another location that night, we did the next best thing to protect ourselves: while I distracted the clerk at the front desk, one of my companions shuffled the white cards in the registry so that no one could figure out which rooms had been assigned to us. (Frankly, it didn't occur to me until much later that the bad guys might have returned to visit us and would have gone into the room of an unsuspecting patron, thinking that the shuffled room assignment cards were accurate. Fortunately that didn't happen.) The next day, we moved to a hotel across the street from the Sangli police station, which was several miles away.

This decision perhaps foretold that the next twenty-four hours would be busy ones.

We traveled south to find Darja, a girl whom we had helped rescue from Karishma's red-light district of Prem Nagar in Miraj. The system had failed Darja. Although we knew she was underage, the judge had "determined" that she was over eighteen. He had released her into the custody of her parents, ignoring the fact that a brothel girl's parents are often complicit in her being sold to the brothel. We wanted to get proof of this girl's real age and to see whether she was still living in her home village.

Our first stop was the school in Darja's home region that she most likely would have attended. It was a government-run school located well into the bush, far from any civilization. This is the school where the poorest of the poor in this remote tribal area send their children. Comprised of six rooms, the school had no windows, chairs or tables. The concrete floors were covered from wall to wall with children sitting and listening to their teachers. Each room held perhaps a hundred or more children.

At the school, we met with the headmaster, who retrieved records from a few years back. The school had no computers or even typewritten records, but rather yellowed sheets of paper recording handwritten lists of children who had attended the school. Although the headmaster searched through the lists diligently, he found no record of Darja's attendance.

The absence of school records for Darja meant that we had lost one source of documentation for her age, and that was disappointing. However, it did give us a little more insight into the life of this victimized girl: her family did not even give her the opportunity for a rudimentary education and she was undoubtedly illiterate. It was time to go to her village and try to find her.

Now, you have to understand that in the tribal areas in South India, there are no addresses. Instead, finding a certain place is a function of asking villagers where a particular person lives. If they want you to know, they will give you directions. If they are suspicious or do not want you to find the person, you will be driving in circles long enough for your clothes to go out of style.

I guess we came across as acceptable, because, thankfully, we did get directions to the village where Darja had been known to live. From the main body of the village, we traveled several more miles into the bush to a collection of about twenty huts where Darja's family was supposed to dwell. As we got out of the car, the villagers quickly gathered around us. We asked for Darja and showed her picture, so that the locals would be sure to know who we were talking about.

At last, reluctantly, someone directed us to her family hut, a tiny thatched-roof structure. Darja wasn't there or anywhere else in the village. Like Karishma, she had seemingly vanished. Her mother and some other family members, however, were present. When we asked what had become of Darja, they finally admitted that she was back in Sangli as a prostitute. She had been retrafficked by her own blood relations for a payment of around $40 from the same brothel owner who had been arrested before.

Searching for trafficking victim, Darja, we did not find her in her remote village. We did, however, find her sister, pictured here in the foreground, and her mother, in the green sari.

This is the village home of Darja. Any caseworker who visited the village should have seen immediately that this was an unsuitable home.

Meanwhile, the mood of the crowd was turning ugly. One of the young men showed up brandishing a rusty knife with a ten-inch blade, and other young men had sticks in hand, threatening us. White people never go to this area, and so the people realized they were in trouble. Theirs was an example of a poor community that had a tradition of trafficking its children, and they were going to do whatever it took to protect themselves. Since we had found out all we could, we got in our car and left.

On the way back to Sangli, we took stock of what our trip had accomplished. We hadn't found Darja. Nor did we have proof of her age. But, we knew where she probably was. Furthermore, we had shown that the government social workers had not done their job in investigating the home situation to which Darja had been returned. Nor had the judge done as he should have by conducting a home inspection. If he had, it would have been clear that Darja's family would not provide a safe environment for her. If someone had reported the true facts about that village to the judge, he could not have sent Darja back there. We would have to do some more investigating to try to find her and get her into a place of safety at last.

We got back to Sangli, and that night one of the investigators who had been with us in Kolhupur received a phone call from a girl of twelve who had overheard her parents in the next room negotiating her sale to a brothel in Mumbai for $200. In this case, the knowledge about the fact that there were people who were out to protect these little ones worked to her favor, as this girl knew who to call for help. The investigator took our driver and advocate and rescued her at a bus stop where they had arranged to meet.

The next day we sent Pranit into Gokul Nagar, Sangli. That was when (as described in chapter five) he was spotted by Kamala Bai and the mob attacked him and then the rest of us. We had to leave town shortly afterward, because the situation had become too hot. I'm deeply sorry to say that we never found Darja or managed to rescue her for a second time. Like Karishma, she is one who got away.

You win some and you lose some in this business. As long as you're in the business of finding and exposing the truth, those who benefit from keeping the truth buried are going to do their best to frustrate your efforts. That doesn't make us quit; it just makes us determined to be that much smarter about what we are doing and more persistent in doing it. And most of the time, we are successful in dragging the dark truth out into the light of day.

After our initial investigations into the presence of an underage girl caught in the flesh trade has produced sufficient evidence, we can then move on to the next stage: intervention. We go in and we get her out.

SEVEN
Going In

The sex trade had gone on undisturbed in Sangli, India, for longer than anyone can tell. That was all about to change on May 20, 2005.

That night, sixty policemen, seventeen female police constables, and eight officers of the Sangli police force took part in a concerted raid upon brothels in the red-light district of Gokul Nagar, intending to pull out underage girls who were being forced to prostitute themselves. Some of the police, mounted on motorcycles, secured the lanes leading into the area so that no one could get in or out during the rescue. Meanwhile, Restore International personnel led police officers to brothels that they, in a survey, had identified two days earlier as housing minor girls in violation of Indian law. Two other Restore operatives were already inside the brothel district as undercover backup, posing as prostitution customers in order to help ensure that the identified girls would not be missed by the police.

The bosses of the sex business in Gokul Nagar had never been troubled by the police before. In fact, some of the police officers were familiar to them as customers of the girls and women in the brothels. Other officers were in the habit of collecting bribes from brothel owners in exchange for turning a blind eye to illegal activities taking place there. Certainly no police raid had ever taken place in the area to shut down prostitution. But this time a courageous district superintendent of police, Milind Bharambe, had listened to our team member about his findings and had given the go-ahead for a large-scale rescue operation.

When the police arrived on the night of the rescue, the residents of Gokul Nagar at first were not sure of what was going on. As the truth dawned on them, many protested loudly. There was little they could do as police officers and Restore staffers searched each of the targeted brothels and rounded up everybody they thought should go into official custody. In less than an hour, the search-and-rescue activities were over.

Having brought buses with them, the police loaded up men, women, and girls. In all, the police gathered up thirteen brothel owners and fourteen johns caught in the act of paying for sex. The police also removed thirty-five women and girls who had been working as prostitutes and who either appeared to be underage or who expressed a desire to leave.[1] They all headed for the police station, where the legal complaint against the brothel owners could be formally lodged, leading to a judge's sorting out of what should happen to each of the people whom the police had collected.

Thus, with a single swift intervention by police and Restore International workers, the complacency of bosses in the Sangli red-light district was broken up. Indeed, a raid on such a scale, reported widely in the papers and on television after it occurred, grabbed the attention of the entire city and beyond. (And the printing of the names of the arrested customers in the newspapers no doubt led to many red faces and caused a number of men to have second thoughts about going into Gokul Nagar.) More importantly, those who ran the sex trade at Gokul Nagar were put on notice that they could no longer expect to carry out illegal activities with impunity. The proof that they got the message came not longer after, when the sex-work bosses organized a public protest over what had happened.

The magnitude of the number of people in flesh trade in Sangli and surrounding areas is enormous. Counting the Gokul Nagar brothel owners, brothel workers, and associated riffraff, there are probably a thousand or more persons involved. This huge number of brothel owners, pimps, and prostitutes from Gokul Nagar marched on the Sangli Police Station and elsewhere to protest disruption of their trade due to the rescue of underage girls. At the end of their march, they gathered in an open area (sort of like a parade ground) before the District Collectors Office, shouting, chanting, and waving signs for hours. To get a sense of the audacity of the sex-trade bosses in staging this protest, realize that this would be like the crooks in your town marching on city hall because the police had dared to arrest some of them—imagine!

This protest goes to show the power of those running the sex trade in the area. They had run this part of the city. They were the ones with the power. They wanted to show the police and other authorities that they called the shots over whether little girls would be sold to twenty customers a day. Not so anymore. A new day had dawned in the Sangli area. No longer could the bosses be confident that their trade would remain undisturbed if they earned their rupees off the sexual servitude of kids . Our raid had gotten the attention of the bad guys.

It had also gained some attention for the bad guys that they would come to regret.

The number of people in the flesh trade is astounding. They run the city and call the shots. In the summer of 2005, brothel owners, pimps, and prostitutes marched on the Sangli District Collectors Office to protest disruption of their trade due to the rescue of underage girls.

Funding the Bad Guys

At the primary entrance to the Gokul Nagar red-light district in Sangli, beside the main street, is a sign listing local members of a nongovernmental organization called VAMP. Ostensibly, this is an organization intended to protect and aid sex workers. So a visitor might be misled into thinking that the message of the sign is that someone is looking out for the well-being of the prostitutes in the area. But, when you realize that the membership of the this organization is largely made up of brothel owners, you realize that this sign is in essence telling passersby who is in charge in Gokul Nagar.

It's like a lawless town in a movie about the Wild West where the bad guys are running the show. In fact, of the brothel keepers arrested in the raid, two of them—Bhimavva Durgappa Gollar and Padma Hanmant Koli—I understand were members of VAMP. Like the others, they were brought up on charges of violating India's anti-prostitution laws.[2] Beyond putting them in hot water legally, the rescue operation took a toll on the bad guys' finances and reputation.

VAMP got its start as a group called SANGRAM (short for Sampada Grameen Mahila Sanstha), which began working in India's Maharashtra and Karnataka states in 1992, distributing condoms to prostitutes and educating these women and girls about HIV/AIDS as well as other sexually transmitted diseases. In 1996 the group broadened into a collective of prostitutes and others called Veshya AIDS Muqabla Parishad (VAMP) who—in their own words—work to "consolidate a common identity among the women and empower them to find their own solutions."[3] The group (which uses both the SANGRAM name and the VAMP name) is essentially pro-prostitution.

This organization seems to publicly blow hot and cold on child prostitution.[4] On the one hand, they offer surface condemnation; on the other hand, they seem to openly promote child prostitution. What is uncontroverted is that the VAMP collective in Gokul Nagar harbored many little girls whose bodies were being sold by those in the area for money. The existence and identity of the young girls in the brothels was certainly not a news flash for the VAMP members, so regardless of the lip service they gave to whether child prostitution was appropriate, the fact was, the kids were there, and their flesh was being sold many times a day. How could any human, any group stand by and watch this happen?

No one is saying that SANGRAM/VAMP doesn't have the right to promote whatever viewpoint it favors. That's what freedom of speech is all about. Here's where it gets sticky: through our investigations, we were shocked to discover that SANGRAM/VAMP was getting some of its funding from you and me, the American taxpayers!

"How could that happen?" you might ask. According to records we acquired, sometime in the late 1990s officials from USAID (the United States Agency for International Development) helped form a joint U.S.-India agency called AVERT. This entity ended up serving as a pass-through entity that sent funds to SANGRAM/VAMP. It seems unusual for USAID to take an indirect route like this in giving money to the NGOs it supports.

No doubt the SANGRAM/VAMP leaders enjoyed the availability of U.S. funding and grew used to receiving the funds that they were allotted. But, they must have been alarmed with the changes to the 2000 anti-trafficking law approved by the U.S. Congress in December 2003 to make it unlawful to distribute U.S. funds to groups that promote, support, or advocate the legalization or practice of prostitution.[5] Other Bush Administration directives contained the same restriction. In fact, USAID's own policy states, "Organizations advocating prostitution as an employment choice or which advocate or support the legalization of prostitution are not appropriate partners for USAID antitrafficking grants or contracts."[6] How then, we asked, was it that our foreign aid was going to this group?

Realizing that the Bush Administration had taken the position that prostitution inherently creates an environment encouraging human trafficking, SANGRAM/VAMP leaders came out against the President publicly. Along with numerous international co-signers who shared their liberal attitude toward prostitution, they added their name to a May 18, 2005, open letter to President Bush, criticizing his position on prostitution.[7] Meanwhile, SANGRAM/VAMP was about to come up against a certain courageous U.S. congressman.

Representative Mark E. Souder, chairman of the Congressional Subcommittee on Criminal Justice, Drug Policy, and Human Resources, and his staff were determined to ensure that USAID abided by its own policy of withholding funding from any organization that promoted prostitution. On two occasions, in October 2004 and July 2005, Congressman Souder and his staff requested information from USAID about the NGOs it was financially supporting, and both times he received inadequate responses from the agency. The pressure on USAID was building.

In September 2005, USAID finally cut funding from SANGRAM/ VAMP—an action that apparently represented the first time it had withheld monies from any organization based on the new anti-prostitution policy. Soon thereafter, Representative Souder wrote a widely reported letter criticizing James Kunder, the USAID assistant administrator for Asia and the Near East, for being so slow to implement the agency's policy and for failing to adequately supply information to Souder's congressional subcommittee.[8]

In his letter, Souder pointed out that USAID for some time had posted on its Web site a report from SANGRAM/VAMP that stated:

We believe that when involuntary initiation into prostitution occurs, a process of socialization within the institution of prostitution exists, whereby the involuntary nature of the business changes increasingly into one of active acceptance, not necessarily with resignation. This is not a coercive process.[9]

Of course it's coercive! This is talking about the process whereby a little girl is abducted, repeatedly raped, and emotionally and physically beaten down until she no longer attempts to resist her sex slavery. That hardly deserves the label of "socialization"—yet this claim was posted on a U.S. government Web site.

Thankfully, some get it. Ambassador John R. Miller, director of the Office to Monitor and Combat Trafficking in Persons, spoke to an Indian newspaper in the wake of the cutoff of funding to SANGRAM/VAMP. He stated, "If the US is going to play a leadership role in abolishing this modern-day slavery in the 21st century, then we need to ensure that US funds go to support that effort and not frustrate it."[10]

Following the Restore-initiated rescue operation in Sangli, I was in close contact on a number of occasions with Marc Wheat, knowledgeable, talented and energetic staff director and chief Counsel for the Committee Chairman Congressman Souder. I had seen SANGRAM/VAMP's true colors by this time, and I knew that Representative Souder was concerned about USAID practices and believed he would be an ally of anyone who found funding of SANGRAM/VAMP to be offensive. That was exactly how it turned out, as Souder shared my concerns and affirmed what Restore International was doing in India. In fact, in his letter to James Kunder, Souder specifically referred to our Sangli raid, pointing out that afterward SANGRAM/VAMP "allowed a brothel keeper into a shelter to pressure the girls not to cooperate with counselors. The girls are now back in the brothels, being subjected to rape for profit."[11]

The fact is, when it came to SANGRAM/VAMP, the United States was funding the bad guys. This supposedly socially responsible group is actually in part made up of people who earn their living from the flesh trade. It is riddled with brothel keepers, many of whom sell the sexual services of teen or preteen girls. And we Americans were handing over our tax dollars to them! Somehow someone was asleep at the switch and had not monitoring what was really going on.

But, there is still more to the story. Not only did Restore help to get funding cut from SANGRAM/VAMP, but also, indirectly, we helped shed daylight on the entire U.S. federal grant process. Here's how it happened.

    Legislators in both houses of the federal legislature introduced bills in the spring of 2006 requiring full disclosure of all entities and organizations receiving federal funds. The plan was for the creation of a Web site where any member of the public could find out where all government grant money is going. And what was one of the instances cited for the need for such a law? USAid funding of SANGRAM/VAMP for which Restore International's intervention in Sangli was mentioned in the *Congressional Record* discussion of the Senate bill.[12] Both bills were unanimously passed in their respective houses, and on September 26, 2006, President George W. Bush signed the Federal Funding and Accountability Transparency Act of 2006.[13]

    When you stir a pot of sludge, unpleasant things come floating to the surface. And in the same way, when we go into dens of prostitution to rescue imprisoned girls, associated evils, such as the hypocrisy of an Indian NGO and the irresponsibility of a U.S. government agency, come to light. This makes the work both scarier and more important. Going in with the simple intention of helping needy girls, we may be able to help clean up more wrongdoing than we even knew existed and bring accountability far beyond the limits of our own work.

Displayed at the entrance to the Gokul Nagar red-light district in Sangli, India, this sign lists local members of VAMP. Two of the people listed on the sign were members of the committee heading up VAMP and were arrested in a Restore International–instigated raid on Gokul Nagar.

On September 26, 2006, President Bush signed into law the Federal Funding and Accountability Transparency Act of 2006, providing for public access to information about all federal grants. Restore International's conflict with SANGRAM/VAMP, an Indian organization with pro-prostitution leanings, was one factor cited as a reason for creating this new law.

To the Rescue

Conducting rescue operations for young girls in Indian brothels is hardly a strategy that Restore International invented. Sometimes the police will go in on their own.[14] And beyond that, other international and homegrown NGOs have been instigating rescue operations of the same sort in India for years. For example, businessmen Vinod Gupta and Sanjay Chonkar, through their organization, Savdhan, have released more than eighty-five hundred young women from coerced prostitution by means of rescues.[15] The International Justice Mission has been doing an outstanding job as well. We ourselves have conducted numerous rescue operations, releasing many girls from their sexual servitude in just our first two years of existence. This has occurred not just in India, but in Uganda as well. When Restore's people have gone into a brothel for a rescue, therefore, we have followed well-settled protocols, which are adapted and practice by many of the best NGOs, enabling an operation that is safe, legal, and—most of all—effective.

Every rescue is different, but the following is generally how rescues are conducted:

Rescues usually take place at night. It's true that the darkness might give perpetrators a better chance to hide or to get away, perhaps taking some of their captives with them, but nighttime is when the brothels are most active. The brothel keepers, pimps, and prostitutes are all on the job. The red-light district is crowded with customers. At night there are more opportunities to verify illegal activity and there are more people around to arrest.

On the night of a typical rescue, the first move is to send in investigators as bogus customers to engage the minor girls we are hoping to release from their captivity. There is a real risk of an underage girl being whisked away by her keeper as soon rumors of a raid starting racing through the brothel district, as inevitably will happen. But, if one of the investigators is actually in the presence of a targeted girl at the time when the rescue party is charging into the area, he may be able to keep her there to be rescued. Furthermore, if the investigator has managed to catch on videotape his transaction with the brothel keeper, this becomes further evidence to convince the police to take the girl into protective custody and to arrest the perpetrator.

The next step is to seal the exits from a brothel or from the area where a brothel is located. Again, in doing this, the objective is to prevent girls being whisked away at the last minute. At least one police officer or staff worker is assigned to guard each exit. The guards prevent unauthorized persons from leaving or entering the premises until the rescue operation is over and all alleged perpetrators have been rounded up.

Once the exits are sealed, the rescue team—made up of both police officers and members of the NGO—go into a brothel. They go in quietly, but their presence quickly stirs up a ruckus when people in the brothel realize what is going on. Some become belligerent and get into the faces of the rescue team to object to what is going on. Others get scared and start to run and hide. This is the riskiest point, since one can't be sure of exactly what will happen.

The police don't know who the people in the brothels are, so they take charge of everybody and begin a sorting-out process. Who is a brothel keeper or a pimp? Who is a prostitute, and does she appear to be under the age of eighteen? Who is a customer? Who might be an innocent bystander (such as a cook hired to prepare food for those captive there)? Who do the children belong to? The questioning starts at once.

Meanwhile, others in the rescue team start a thorough search of the place, because what meets the eye is not always everything there is. Some brothel owners, knowing the risk of being raided, have prepared hiding places in advance and stuff their minor girls in there at the first sign of trouble. So it is important to look for signs of occupation or disorder, such as shoes or clothes in strange places or furniture out of place, as this might indicate that someone has ducked into a hiding place. Searchers check the thickness of walls to see if there is unaccounted for space. They examine mirrors to see if they might be masking an entrance to a hiding place. They look under beds, search attics and crawl spaces, and poke around everywhere until it is clear that everybody who is there has been located.

The focus during the raid, of course, is the minor girls. These girls are often bewildered and frightened when a small army of police and investigators pour into their home and start rounding people up. They wonder, *What's happening? Am I going to get into trouble?* It is important to make sure there is at least one female staff member who can engage the girls in conversation while the raid is in process and offer reassurance. She gives them the good news that—as scary as the rescue might seem—this is actually their chance to come out of a life of prostitution and perhaps eventually go home. She answers whatever questions they might have and calms their fears. The girls may not understand or believe her at this point, but at least they are beginning to get the idea that the rescue operation is meant to help them and not harm them.

The searching can take a while, but once it is complete, the police round up everybody who is a suspect and cart them off to jail. Since in India being a prostitute is not illegal, but running a prostitution business is, the police do not necessarily take the prostitutes themselves into custody. This can be a problem if it means the police overlook minor girls. So it is important to make sure they have charge of all those girls who appear to be under the age of eighteen or who wish to leave the brothel. The adult prostitutes who show no desire to leave the brothel are generally left alone. All the perpetrators—the brothel keepers, managers, pimps, and customers caught in the act—are pointed out and the officers are asked to take them to the police station for questioning.

Those conducting the raid with authorities accompany the police and the brothel personnel back to the police station. They try to separate the girls from the perpetrators to head off attempts to intimidate the girls into refusing to testify against the perpetrators. If possible, they also separate the young girls from the older, more hardened prostitutes, who might likewise be a negative influence upon them. They see that steps are taken to remand the girls to a government-run home, as stipulated in Indian law, so that they can begin receiving aftercare.

That's what it's all about: giving girls a chance to lead normal lives again.

In Defense of Rescues

We don't charge into red-light districts with police on motorcycles and paddy wagons, barging into brothels and rounding up wrongdoers, because we get a thrill out of it. We have no illusions that we are marshals riding in to clean up a Wild West town taken over by desperadoes. If anyone is playing that role, it is the Indian police; we are just the instigators and the ones who go along to make sure the work is done well. The truth is, the brothels of India are terrible places, and if it were merely a matter of our own preference, we would never go near them. We do it for the girls.

Let's not forget, these girls are captives. They may not be physically restrained (though, then again, some are), yet through the fiction of debt bondage or another ruse, they are trapped in a situation that robs them of liberty, health, and hope for a good life. If someone doesn't advocate for them, if someone doesn't call attention to the wrong, they will stay right where they are there until they die, quite possibly in the near future.[16] Furthermore, our experience in places like Sangli and Miraj (where Karishma was exploited) shows that even a few interventions through the appropriate police stations will create a high level of deterrence, discouraging traffickers from exploiting other young girls.

Harriet Tubman snuck into the American South repeatedly to put slaves aboard the Underground Railroad, and in the same way we have to go into brothels and pull the girls out. It's legal; it's necessary; and we plan to do it again and again in various countries where we operate, as often as innocent kids are being sacrificed to the flesh trade.

After the rescue operation, there is much left to be done and, from this point on, our work travels along two parallel tracks, one related to the perpetrators and the other related to the victims. We attempt to see that the captors of young girls are tried, convicted, and punished, and we strive to ensure that the girls are given every possible chance to be restored to wholeness and begin a new life.

EIGHT

Putting the Bad Guys Behind Bars

Restore International Strategy Part 3—Legal Action

The raid on the Gokul Nagar red-light district in Sangli, India, was over in less than an hour; the legal wrangling that has followed is still not finished. And the mixed results of the legal follow-up illustrate both the good intentions and the flawed implementation of the Indian legal system when it comes to protecting children from sexual exploitation and punishing their exploiters.

As soon as the buses pulled up at the Sangli police station on the night of the raid with Gokul Nagar personnel inside, one of our Indian investigators, Sarthak Kamla, filed a First Information Report (FIR), which is required when a crime is alleged. The police then filled out their charge sheet, officially initiating the criminal proceedings against the suspects on the basis of the Immoral Trafficking (Prevention) Act.[1] The fourteen customers were charged with hiring prostitutes—a minor (though embarrassing) offense.[2] The thirteen brothel keepers were charged with keeping a brothel, living on the earnings of a prostitute, procuring a person for the sake of prostitution, and detaining a person in premises where prostitution is carried on.[3] And the thirty-five prostitutes were charged with having carried out prostitution and with soliciting for the purpose of prostitution.[4]

In short order, all the prostitutes, brothel keepers, and customers were hauled up before a judge, who had stayed late at work that night for this purpose. In this initial hearing, he determined what should be done with all of the people whom the police had gathered up at Gokul Nagar. He ordered that the customers be released and stand trial at a future date. He ordered that the brothel keepers be kept in custody pending a bail hearing. And he ordered that the prostitutes be kept in police custody as well until it could be determined which ones were minors and which were adults.

So far, all was in order, but the very next day, our attempts to ensure that justice would be done began to be challenged. It started with the age verification process.

According to Indian legal precedent, underage prostitutes (those younger than eighteen) are not to be tried for the crime of prostitution, but instead are to be turned over to the local Child Welfare Committee. So to determine which of the thirty-five prostitutes in custody were minors, they all were sent to the Sangli Civil Hospital the day after the raid for age verification. (This is typical in such cases. Many times, these girls don't possess copies of their birth certificates or even know how old they are, or if they do, they may have been instructed by their brothel keepers to claim to be eighteen or older.)[5] The results were inconclusive and demanded a further, more accurate assessment.

Just by looking at the prostitutes who had been gathered up, our people could tell that a large number of them were under eighteen. They also knew that it is common in India for doctors to inflate the ages of prostitutes they are examining. In fact, one government study looked into several cases where this occurred and concluded, "The disturbing fact is that in all these cases, the second examination showed the person to be younger than what was supposedly found in the earlier examination. Sometimes, the difference is unbelievable. Since the technology used for age verification is very advanced and cannot be dismissed as subjective and imperfect, the fault obviously lies with the people applying the technology."[6] It's hard to know when the doctors are merely being inept and when they are sympathetic to the brothel keepers (or perhaps have even been offered a bribe to adjust the results).

With the prostitutes released from Gokul Nagar, we requested and were granted a repetition of the age verification process. This time the medical examiner determined that eight girls were under the age of seventeen and that nine more were between the ages of seventeen and nineteen. Since the precise ages of the nine older girls could not be determined, the court order assigning the juveniles into the care of the Child Welfare Committee stated that it was in their best interest for the legal system to consider them all as minors. And that's what was done. All seventeen girls were placed in the Sangli Remand Home.

Meanwhile, an advocate (lawyer) showed up in court on the day after the raid for the bad guys. First, he applied for bail on behalf of the thirteen brothel keepers. He also disputed the minor status of the girls, presenting birth certificates that made them out to be over the age of eighteen. Incredibly, by these actions, he was purporting to represent both the brothel keepers and the young girls who were their captives. That's like an attorney trying to represent both the defense and the prosecution sides of the same case!

The advocate's efforts met with partial success. Against our objections, the judge agreed with his request to grant the brothel keepers bail, allowing these alleged perpetrators to leave police custody. Fortunately, when it came to the status of the girls, the judge took the evidence of the second medical examination instead of the claims of this lawyer, and he directed that all seventeen of the minor girls remain in the government home.

Before long, we learned an interesting fact about this advocate. A court order from the CWC linked the advocate with the director of SANGRAM, the NGO that started VAMP. This is the collective dominated by brothel owners and others who make their living off the sex trade—the same group that organized a protest against Restore in Sangli. It's no wonder, then, that the advoctae was trying to protect the brothel keepers and to put the young girls back into their clutches. And he didn't give up. He went on to apply for the release of fifteen of the seventeen minor girls at the Child Welfare Committee and later at the Judicial Magistrates Court.

We consistently opposed the advocate's efforts to put minor girls back in a position where others can force them to prostitute themselves. In particular, we wanted to dig deeper into the birth certificates that this officer of the court had submitted and that appeared fishy to us, to say the least. In this we were successful.

With a lot of hard work, we were able to track down school records for some of the girls that established their real ages as being under eighteen. By comparing school documents, we even found that some of the falsified birth certificates that had been submitted to the court contained information that pertained to other, older girls, not to the ones who had been forced to prostitute themselves. In other cases, it appeared, the information on the forged birth certificates had simply been made up.

ಕರ್ನಾಟಕ ಸರ್ಕಾರ
Government of Karnataka
ಜನನ ಮತ್ತು ಮರಣಗಳ ಮುಖ್ಯ ರಿಜಿಸ್ಟ್ರಾರ್
Chief Registrar of Births and Deaths

ನಮೂನೆ ನಂ. 5
(8 ನೇ ನಿಯಮ ನೋಡಿ)
FORM No. 5
(See Rule 8)
ಜನನ ಪ್ರಮಾಣ ಪತ್ರ
(12/17 ನೇ ಪ್ರಕರಣ ಮೇರೆಗೆ ಕೊಡಲಾದ)
BIRTH CERTIFICATE
(Issued Under Section 12/17)

ಈ   ಕೆಳಕಂಡ   ಒಿವರಗಳನ್ನು   ಕರ್ನಾಟಕ   ರಾಜ್ಯದ ....ಜಿಲ್ಲೆಯ

....   ತಾಲ್ಲೂಕಿನ   ....(ಗ್ರಾ/ಪ/ಪಟ್ಟಣ)

ರಿಜಿಸ್ಟರಿನಲ್ಲಿರುವ ಜನನ ಸಂಬಂಧವಾದ ಮೂಲ ದಾಖಲೆಯಿಂದ ತೆಗೆದುಕೊಳ್ಳಲಾಗಿದೆಯೆಂದು ಪ್ರಮಾಣೀಕರಿಸಲಾಗಿದೆ.

This is to certify that the following information has been taken from the
original record of birth which is the register for *Muddapur* (village/town) of
Mudhol taluk, of *Bagalkot* district of Karnataka State.

(1) ಹೆಸರು
    Name ▓▓▓▓▓

(2) ತಂದೆಯ ಹೆಸರು
    Name of Father ▓▓▓▓▓▓▓

(3) ಲಿಂಗ
    Sex *Female*

(4) ತಾಯಿಯ ಹೆಸರು
    Name of Mother ▓▓▓▓▓▓▓

(5) ಜನನವಾದ ತಾರೀಖು
    Date of Birth *10-12-1986*

(6) ನೋಂದಣೆ ಸಂಖ್ಯೆ
    Registration No. *23*

(7) ಜನನವಾದ ಸ್ಥಳ
    Place of Birth *Mudd...*

(8) ...ತಾರೀಖು
    Date of Registration *10/12/1986*

Date:

Signature of Issuing Authority

Seal :

WD-1678 - 1500 PAD - GSPB

*An example of the sort of birth certificates Restore International proved to
have been falsified in order to make underage prostitutes appear older than
they were.*

We will likely run up against the same people again when our
advocate appears in court for the trial of the brothel keepers—if that ever
occurs. In India, the period of time between the commission of a crime and
the trial of the alleged perpetrator runs somewhere between a very long time
and never. And of course, the longer it takes for this trial, the harder it will be

to assemble witnesses ready to testify against the brothel owners. What we ultimately want to see is the brothel keepers who traffic and abuse little girls in violation of their countries' laws stashed behind bars and their brothels left standing empty.

Child Prostitution and the Law

Forcing girls to prostitute themselves is not only a sin and tragedy; it is also a *crime*, a prosecutable offense. So after we rescue underage girls from brothels in India and elsewhere, we do everything we can to see that the perpetrators are arrested, tried, and punished. Indeed, we have found that legal action against the perpetrators is the single most important element in producing widespread and lasting change. Why? Because as those running the sex trade see some of their own going to jail for violating laws against trafficking in children, they have second thoughts about engaging in the same criminal activity. They know that law enforcement agencies and the courts will no longer tolerate child prostitution, and they realize that they might be the next to wind up in prison.

Restore staffers do not prosecute perpetrators; public prosecutors do that, but we are able to support the prosecution process at several points, helping to see that the guilty are punished. Since not all public prosecutors are well versed in the laws that apply to child prostitution, we help them to understand these laws better. We check to make sure that the rescued girls have been put into safe custody, as provided for in the national law. We request that law enforcement officers shut down the raided brothels. At the bail hearing for the perpetrators, we make an appearance to oppose bail. We organize witnesses and take statements from rescued girls in order to give the prosecutors ammunition during the trial. And when we feel that a perpetrator has either been acquitted unfairly or given too light a sentence, we appeal the case to a higher court.

All of this requires that we understand and effectively apply the relevant laws. And in fact, in our experience, the Indian laws are mostly adequate for the case, starting with the country's most basic legal document. The Constitution of India declares, "Traffic in human beings ... and other similar forms of forced labour are prohibited and any contravention of this provision shall be an offence punishable in accordance with law."[7] This is a clear and forthright statement, putting India on the right side of the modern-day slavery problem in principle.

Reflecting the Constitution, the Indian Penal Code (IPC) enumerates several specific human trafficking violations and provides for penalties. Among the slavery and slavery-related violations of law that the Penal Code identifies are the following crimes:

- abducting a woman and forcing or seducing her into illicit intercourse
- forcing or seducing any girl under the age of eighteen into illicit intercourse
- abducting any person and subjecting that person to "grievous hurt, or slavery, or to the unnatural lust of any person"
- buying or disposing of any person as a slave
- selling or buying any person under the age of eighteen for purposes of prostitution

The punishment for each of these crimes is a fine and up to ten years in prison.[8]

In addition to the Penal Code, the two most important legal documents relating to the crime of child prostitution in India are the Immoral Traffic (Prevention) Act (1956, amended 1986) and the Juvenile Justice (Care and Protection of Children) Act (1986, amended 2001).

The Immoral Traffic (Prevention) Act (ITPA) has been on the books for half a century and is the legal remedy Indian prosecutors refer to most in their trials against alleged perpetrators of child prostitution, as in the case at Sangli. This act clearly makes it a crime to force a person to become a prostitute. It also criminalizes facilitating prostitution, such as brothel keeping, living off the earnings of prostitutes, and procuring customers for prostitutes, even where sex work is not coerced.[9]

The ITPA was amended in 1986 to provide for more severe penalties for offenses involving children and minors. Under this act, anyone who detains a girl with the intent that she have sexual intercourse with other persons is liable to punishment. To assist in prosecution, certain circumstances are presumed to constitute illegal detainment. For example, if someone is found with a child in a brothel, or if a child who has been sexually assaulted is found in a brothel, it is presumed that the child has been illegally detained. The penalty for inducing someone to engage in prostitution is imprisonment from seven years to life when the victim is under the age of sixteen and from seven to fourteen years when he or she is sixteen or seventeen years old. A court is, however, allowed to impose a lower sentence for special reasons.

A drawback of the ITPA is that it criminalizes solicitation for prostitution. (Prostitution itself is not prohibited under the law, but public soliciting for prostitution is.) This has led to the arrest and punishment of girls who had been forced by brothel owners to solicit. A government study reported, "In many places, the percentage of trafficked victims to the total number of 'sex workers' added up to more than 90 per cent. Therefore, it is the trafficked victim who usually gets detained [under section 8] of the ITPA. This means that more often than not, the law is used to criminalize the woman/girl who has been arrested, despite the fact that she is usually a trafficking victim. The crime of trafficking has remained suppressed under the alleged crime of soliciting. This is, in fact, a violation of the basic rights of women and children."[10]

We agree—this is unfair. And in fact, there have been cases where police have used the law to arrest prostitutes as a means of preventing them from being rescued. The police then return the girls to their brothel keepers. Surely this is a travesty of the intent of the law! Thankfully, India's Inter-Ministerial Committee on Trafficking in Persons has drafted revisions to the ITPA that would eliminate the criminalization of solicitation, and the committee has submitted these revisions to the Indian Parliament for consideration.

Along with the ITPA, at least one other Indian law—the Juvenile Justice Act (JJA)—often comes into play in courtroom cases after minor girls are rescued. The JJA does a good job of establishing standards for juvenile justice in the areas of investigation, prosecution, and adjudication. It also provides well for rehabilitation and treatment for neglected juveniles. Its weakness is in the modest criminal penalties it invokes for sex offenses against minors—a fine and six

Laws Affecting Human Trafficking

India

In India, laws against forced labor in general, and sex trafficking in particular, are generally adequate, though they carry sentences that are too light.

• THE IMMORAL TRAFFICKING (PREVENTION) ACT (1956, 1986) — criminalizes the selling of women and children for commercial sex and profiting from prostitution.

• THE ABOLITION OF BONDED LABOR ACT (1976) — abolishes bonded labor and prohibits children under the age of fourteen from doing hazardous labor.

• JUVENILE JUSTICE ACT (1986, 2001) — establishes standards for investigation, prosecution, and adjudication, as well as provides for the rehabilitation of juveniles.

• CHILD LABOR ACT (1986) — regulates the industries in which children under the age of fourteen are permitted to be employed.

(cont'd on next page)

United States

U.S. laws are relevant, not only for human trafficking within the United States, but also for regulating American opposition to trafficking overseas and for assigning foreign nations to the three-tier list of compliance with these laws.

• TRAFFICKING VICTIMS PROTECTION ACT (2000) — defines trafficking in persons and provides enhanced protection, prosecution, and prevention of such trafficking.

• TRAFFICKING VICTIMS PROTECTION REAUTHORIZATION ACT (2003, 2006) — creates a new information campaign to stop sex trafficking, refines the federal criminal law, and provides means for victims to sue traffickers in federal court.

• THE PROTECT ACT (Prosecutorial Remedies and Other Tools to end Exploitation of Children Today Act, 2003) — strengthens law enforcement to prevent, investigate, prosecute, and punish violent crimes committed against children.

(cont'd on next page)

months in jail for cruelty to a juvenile or a fine and three years in jail for exploitation of a juvenile employee.[11]

These laws need not be held separate; law enforcement officials can combine the JJA or the ITPA with the IPC in charging alleged perpetrators. This may cause the trial to take longer, but it also expands the scope of the case against the alleged criminal. For example, if a minor girl is a sex trafficking victim, her exploiters can be charge-sheeted not only under the ITPA, but also under the IPC for rape and other crimes. But, this rarely happens. "The data collected from police officers across the country shows that law enforcement agencies usually do not invoke sections of the IPC, thereby denying justice to the victim and at the same time, allowing culprits to escape."[12]

Whether we are talking about the IPC, the ITPA, or the JJA, the problem is not primarily with the laws; it is with the enforcement.[13]

Arrested and Tried—Maybe, Eventually

Far too few sex traffickers and customers of sex trafficking in India ever come into police custody, much less do jail time for their wrongdoing. According to one government-sponsored investigation, in the years 1997 to 2001, an average of 8,927 crimes were reported under the Immoral Trafficking (Prevention) Act annually. That's a tiny number compared to the total child prostitution problem, but fortunately the numbers were tending to increase year by year during the five-year period, suggesting that law enforcement in this area is gradually improving.[14]

A closer look at the data, however, reveals at least one additional form of injustice. Breaking down the arrest statistics by gender shows that 87 percent of those arrested under the ITPA were women. This suggests that prostitutes and their madams are being arrested fairly frequently, but that the customers are usually being let go free by the police. The report called this example of gender discrimination "a matter of serious concern."[15]

The same report claims that the conviction rate is high for those perpetrators who come to trial, though the cases are often left in limbo for several years. "The reality of the situation is … that 90 per cent of the chargesheeted persons are convicted in due course (though the 'course' may be unduly delayed)."[16] If that number is correct, it makes that much stronger the argument that a real impact could be made upon India's child prostitution problem if the criminals were more vigorously pursued and brought to justice.

Much of the blame for India's child prostitution epidemic is rightly laid at the feet of India's police forces. The police are accused of supporting brothel owners, being in complicity with traffickers, and according the crime of trafficking a low priority. Criticism has been leveled at their conduct during some rescue operations, their behavior toward both perpetrators and victims, the way in which they conduct age verification of rescued prostitutes, and their lack of appropriate networking with other agencies, such as protective homes.[17]

Speaking up in their own defense, the police of India report obstacles to pursuing sex traffickers more vigorously. They fear allegations of victimization by brothel owners who might use their political clout against the police. They find it difficult to send children to juvenile homes due to poor facilities and lack of communication with welfare authorities. They are often seriously

United Nations

Member nations of the United Nations, including India, are expected to abide by UN conventions and protocols related to human trafficking.

• CONVENTION FOR THE SUPPRESSION OF THE TRAFFIC IN PERSONS AND OF THE EXPLOITATION OF THE PROSTITUTION OF OTHERS (1949) — declares that enslaving women and children and forcing them into prostitution is a violation of human rights.

• CONVENTION AGAINST TRANSNATIONAL ORGANIZED CRIME (2000) — promotes international police and judicial cooperation against organized crime (thus indirectly aiding efforts to end trafficking in persons).

• PROTOCOL TO PREVENT, SUPPRESS AND PUNISH TRAFFICKING IN PERSONS, ESPECIALLY WOMEN AND CHILDREN (2000) — defines trafficking in persons, criminalizes trafficking, encourages protection of victims, and promotes prevention

(cont'd on next page)

of trafficking through research, public awareness campaigns, and social and economic initiatives.

• PRINCIPLES AND GUIDELINES ON HUMAN RIGHTS AND HUMAN TRAFFICKING (2002) — offers guidelines for protecting victims and punishing criminals.

understaffed and lacking in resources. And sometimes the victims turn hostile toward them, making them wonder why they should even bother trying to rescue these girls.[18]

In my view, while the police may have some legitimate complaints that ought to be addressed, they do bear responsibility for not pursuing criminals in brothel districts more forcefully. And I am far from alone in this opinion. For example, in 1998, India's Committee on Prostitution, Child Prostitutes and Children of Prostitutes issued its "Plan of Action to Combat Trafficking and Commercial Sexual Exploitation of Women and Children," in which the committee acknowledged that law enforcement had not made much of an impact on the commercial sexual exploitation of women and children. The report cited the following reasons:

- lack of seriousness among law enforcement officers and administrators
- risks faced by social workers, NGOs, and government officials working in red-light districts
- a lack of awareness about the prevalence of child trafficking
- difficulties in estimating the age of child victims
- lack of coordination among border police of neighboring countries to stop cross-border trafficking

Unfortunately, little has changed regarding these problems in India since 1998.[19]

At Restore International, we have personally seen that when the police and courts in a particular area enforce the laws on child sex trafficking, it makes a real difference. For example, the city of Kolhapur, with a population of around half a million, has only a small red-light district, and the investigations I participated in there uncovered not a single minor girl at work. Meanwhile, Sangli, a city of about four hundred thousand persons, has a huge red-light district with many unfortunate girls forced to sell themselves. The difference is that in Kolhapur the police officials are serious about ridding their city of illegal prostitution, while in Sangli many of the police cooperate closely with the brothel keepers.

This is why putting pressure upon law enforcement officers to arrest those involved in child prostitution and to shut down the trade is so important. By consistently exposing the crimes being committed, insisting that police arrest the guilty, and watching to see that courts fulfill their duty to punish wrongdoers, caring persons both from India and from outside can begin to change a legal culture in the country that has for too long turned a blind eye to the forced prostitution of children and teenagers. We work for such change. It will be a good thing for India—and a very good thing for the little girls.

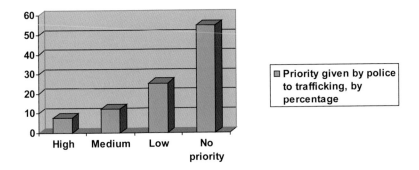

Figure 8.1 Priority given by police to trafficking issues[20]

Putting the *Action* in Legal Action

Because the police and courts in India cannot always be trusted to do the right thing on their own, NGOs like ours have to get involved to prod, guide, and remind them. Experts in the field have developed a protocol by which it is intended that team members will participate in the legal process at key points to make sure that the girls' rights are protected and that justice is served on their exploiters.

At the police station. On the night of the rescue operation, justice workers do their best to look out for the girls' well-being while they are in police custody. They ask the police officers to separate the victims from the accused in order to minimize the brothel keepers intimidation and undue influence upon the girls. They also ask the police, if possible, to separate the young girls from the older, more hardened prostitutes. Finally, they insist that a female police officer or social worker be present when the girls are questioned by officers after the raid, in keeping with section 15 of the Immoral Trafficking (Prevention) Act.

As time permits, immediately after the rescue, they also try to conduct their own interviews with each of the girls separately, since sometimes the girls are more forthcoming at this point than they are later, after their keepers have gotten to them. They take notes on these interviews and make the notes available to the prosecuting legal team. They may get only basic information from the girls at this stage, but they submit whatever they get to the advocate who will be working on the case the following day.

Under India's Code of Criminal Procedure, when a citizen has made a complaint about a crime, a police officer must create a First Information Report (FIR). So, as the complainant in the case, one of the team members asks the police to make a strong case against the perpetrators under sections 3–7 and 9 of the ITPA. If the victims are clearly minor or are readily giving statements against the accused, the complainant encourages the police to add relevant Indian Penal Code sections 366, 366A, 368, 372–373, and 376 to the FIR.

Once the FIR has been created, justice workers wait to make sure that the case is actually charge-sheeted. If it is not, that means the police do not intend to pursue this case any further. They will likely release both the perpetrators and the girls, who will go right back into the brothels. So if it looks like that might happens, the workers contact the senior police officer immediately and ask for assistance. Most of the time, though, if the police have agreed to performing a raid, they will file the case and take it to a judge.

At the judicial hearings. There are usually one or two hearings before a judge early in the legal proceedings—one to determine what will be done with the arrested persons and another to determine bail. The goal at these hearings is to see that the girls are properly protected and that the alleged perpetrators are made to face up to the crimes of which they have been accused.

Many tasks may be necessary in the early hours and days after a raid to ensure that a rescued girl's best interests are represented. Team members ensure that when the rescued girl is remanded before the court and sent for age verification a social worker accompanies her at all times. During court proceedings, the victim girl must be protected from intimidation or false promises and from unscrupulous lawyers appointed by the brothel keepers to regain custody of her. If justice workers suspect that the age verification results have been manipulated, they seek a second opinion. They interact with the probation officer assigned to the underaged girls to monitor the actions that are taken on their behalf.

In the first week or two after a rescue operation, caseworkers compile more detailed statements from the girls for use in the future trial. The caseworkers may need to make repeated visits to the aftercare home during this period to conduct interviews and create the evidentiary statements. Once the statements are complete, the caseworkers see that the girls sign their statements in the presence of the superintendent of the aftercare home, then submit them to the police and court for inclusion in the charge sheet against the accused.

Sometimes interviews with the girls turn up information that could strengthen the case against perpetrators. For instance, their stories may make it possible for the police to add further sections of the law to the case against some of the perpetrators, and so justice workers inform the police of this. Also, the girls might give information that implicates additional people in the crimes committed. In that case, investigators bring this information to the attention of the police and then work with them to track down and arrest the alleged criminals.

Meanwhile, when the bail hearing for the perpetrators comes up, Restore team members work with the public prosecutors in opposing bail. At this point, all available evidence against the accused, including evidence collected during the investigation and statements taken from the girls, is brought before the attention of the court. Team members try to show how serious the case is, in the hopes that the perpetrators will remain behind bars where they cannot continue exploiting children. And in the event that bail is granted anyway, they monitor the situation in case the perpetrators threaten the girls, tamper with evidence, or offer any indication that they might abscond before the trial, and they immediately bring any information of this sort to the attention of the court to prevent a miscarriage of justice.

Before, during, and after the trial. As we have seen, it can take a very long time for a case to come to trial, but the prosecution of the guilty is crucially important, and so the team members stick with it, doing what they can to help throughout the process. In fact, through the legal principle known as *stare decisis*, they can help shape India's legal precedents in dealing with the commercial sexual exploitation of children.

The girls rescued from brothels are victims—but they are also witnesses. While they are in temporary aftercare facilities, and then when they move on to whatever is next for them in life, team members try to keep in touch with them so that they remain available to appear in court once the trial finally occurs. For one thing, they have to make sure that the girls are not pressured by the brothel owners or any representatives of the brothel owners to stay out of the court proceedings. And since many of these girls would prefer to put their past behind them and not drag their degradation out into public, they also keep repeating the importance of their testifying in court so that the criminals may be punished and other girls can be protected.

As the trial draws nearer, members of the team help prepare willing witnesses for their court appearances. This starts with reviewing the statement a victim girl gave to the police.

When the trial comes, the justice workers make sure that the witnesses appear at the right time. They encourage the prosecutor to strongly object to any indecent or irrelevant questions put to the girls. They monitor what is happening during the trial and offer advice and encouragement to the prosecutor as needed. In short, they do whatever they can, within the bounds of laws and morality, to help the trial come to a favorable conclusion.

Hopefully, the trial has a successful conclusion as the sex traffickers are convicted and sentenced to jail time. And as we have seen, although the wait to go to trial is often unconscionably long, when they do take place, convictions are common. And when a guilty verdict is rendered, justice workers go to the police and apply for closure of the brothels belonging to the convicts, as provided for in section 18 of the ITPA. This is a real victory, because it means that the brothel keepers' operations are crippled and they are prevented from trafficking more young girls into sexual servitude.

On the other hand, if the alleged perpetrators are acquitted, team members re-examine the case to determine whether there may be sufficient grounds to appeal the case to a higher court. They also initiate other high court orders as the need arises. In short, they stick with the case as long as possible or necessary to see that justice is done.

The legal process can be frustratingly slow in India, but when we or other justice workers get girls released into the care of social workers, put their exploiters behind bars, and shut down the brothels that imprisoned them, it is all worth it. Making a real difference of this kind is what I dreamed about back when all my legal work involved trading dollars among participants in U.S. court cases. Our efforts at Restore International are literally saving lives.

NINE
The Chance for a New Life
Restore International Strategy Part 4—Aftercare

Seventeen minor girls were rescued from the Gokul Nagar red-light district in Sangli, and immediately the authorities started trying to figure out what should best be done for them. The judge who held the initial hearing after the Gokul Nagar raid followed Indian law by remanding the underage girls to a government-run home in Sangli. This home is nothing special; its facilities are plain and not especially comfortable, but at least the girls were given the basic provisions they needed, such as bed sheets, towels, soap, and clothing, and had a place to stay and food to eat. Most of all, they were free.

At this point, the girls were taken into the care of the local Child Welfare Committee (CWC), which oversees the government home. Not every location in India has a CWC in place, as the law stipulates, but fortunately Sangli does. In addition to providing housing for the girls, the CWC also appointed a probation officer to submit a report regarding the parents of the seventeen girls. This report would determine whether it was safe for the girls to go home, so that a decision could be made about their long-term disposition.

In short, the system was working the way it was supposed to—or at least it seemed to be doing so at first. Cracks in the system began showing quickly. For instance, as mentioned in a U.S. State Department memorandum, one of the brothel keepers from Gokul Nagar managed to get into the home "to pressure the girls not to cooperate with counselors."[1]

Sadly, this emissary from the red-light district was successful in getting some of the girls to go back into prostitution. The home study conducted by the probation officer also did not go as it should have.[2]

The probation officer was supposed to visit each of the home situations for the girls, ask questions, and determine whether it would be safe for the girls to go home. The reality is that, in many cases, it would not be safe for them to return, because their families and villages might reject them. Or their parents, having sold them into prostitution in the first place, might see this as a chance to double their money by reselling a girl to a brothel owner. We don't know how many of the girls' homes this probation officer actually visited, but regardless, this officer didn't do the job well, because over the course of two months she released *all* the girls to their parents. Although at least some of the parents were asked to (and did) promise to prevent their daughters from going back into prostitution, some of the girls soon disappeared, sent back by relatives to sell their bodies for the enrichment of others.[3]

Other of the rescued girls, I am pleased to say, stayed out of the prostitution racket and are leading normal lives now. Some of these have married and all have found healthier ways to make a living. And that's what it's all about: giving girls a chance to lead normal lives again. It's only a shame that the rest of the girls rescued in the raid did not have as good an outcome. We have taken it as a reminder that we must continue striving to make the aftercare system work better for the girls we rescue from the brothels of India.

A Holistic Approach

Rescuing enslaved girls from brothels is not enough. Putting their slaveholders behind bars and shutting down the brothels is not enough either. What happens to the girls *after* they are released from sex slavery? We want them to be not merely released from their captivity, but also restored to as good a life as they can reasonably expect to have. Indeed, having pulled them out of their captivity, we feel a responsibility to see that they are properly cared for until they are adults and can make decisions on their own.

Kevin Bales, a social researcher who focuses upon modern-day slavery, has emphasized the crucial place of aftercare for victims of sex trafficking. "It could be argued that the enslaved prostitutes' need for rehabilitation is generally more profound than that of other freed slaves. All slavery can be a harrowing and traumatizing experience, but the repeated sexual violation amounting to rape that characterizes forced prostitution brings tremendous psychological damage and requires intensive rebuilding of self-esteem and self-worth."[4]

What we have discovered with our efforts in Uganda in particular is that good aftercare is the steppingstone of recovery before rescued girls can successfully live in mainstream society, and the aftercare portion of Restore International's strategy is what makes it truly holistic. As dramatic as undercover investigations and brothel raids are, and as important as prosecution of the offenders is, without proper aftercare, these prior steps are largely useless for changing the lives of the rescued girls for good. And that's why we're looking out for the girls' total welfare, not just their freedom. We're committed. We're involved. We're out for long-term change.

The Indian government has good intentions of providing for children who have been abused and neglected. The Juvenile Justice Act calls for the government to provide homes and assistance for these children, and Child Welfare Committees like the one in Sangli are the primary bodies charged with providing this assistance, under the oversight of the central government's Ministry of Women and Child Development.[5] Once again, it's not the laws that are the problem; it's in the carrying out of them where government agencies all too often fail their citizens. Not all districts of India are equipped to carry out the provisions of the law to protect juveniles, and even when they do, the care they provide is often short term and inadequate.

Just as Restore International supplements the Indian legal system in upholding the laws against child prostitution, so the Indian aftercare system needs to be supplemented in providing for girls rescued from brothels. After all, if these girls don't get adequate care, past history has shown that the odds are as high that they will end up right back where they came from. They might be grabbed by their former brothel owners; they might go home, only to be resold into sex slavery; or they might even return voluntarily to the brothels because they don't know anything else to do. We have to show them that there is a better future for them—and show them how to get there.

When the girls come out of the brothels, they typically are undernourished and have significant health problems, are suffering psychologically from the trauma they have undergone, have no family members who truly care about them, have little education and may be illiterate, have no marketable skills, and don't know how to operate independently. They need a wide range of care and guidance after their release if they are ever to become happy and productive members of their society again. According to the U.S. State Department, rescued victims of trafficking may need translation, housing, food, clothing, medical care, legal assistance, language training, vocational or educational training, and counseling as part of their aftercare.[6] In short, a complete system of aftercare is necessary if the girls are to have their future restored to them.

A Place to Call Home

Most girls working in Indian brothels live in the same tiny quarters where they are forced to ply their trade. They can't go back there once they are rescued, or else they will inevitably reenter prostitution. Where, then, can they live?

Stage one: government remand homes. Initially, and in accordance with the law, rescued girls are sent to a government remand home. These facilities are often understaffed and poorly maintained.[7] They can also be crowded, with the majority of them holding more than one hundred girls at a time.[8] The food served is basic and the girls may sleep on concrete floors. At least the girls are safe here, but they typically don't like staying in these homes. This is usually a difficult time for the rescued girls, a time of adjustment, uncertainty, and discomfort. Sometimes they run away and are lost sight of for good.

The time that a girl spends at a remand home varies considerably, though the average length is from three to six months.[9] During this period, the Child Welfare Committee for the district (often coordinating with an NGO such as Restore International) is responsible for conducting a home study to determine whether it is safe for a child to be returned to her home. A social worker goes to the girl's family home, interviews whomever he or she finds there, and tries to determine whether the girl will be properly taken care of if the committee were to return her into the custody of her family.[10]

The first choice of the government is for the girl to return to her own village and family. This, however, is rarely a good resolution for the rescued girl. In some cases, especially in the rare cases when a girl has been abducted by a stranger, her home environment might be healthy and nurturing and she might be welcomed back with open arms. However, most of the time, family members were the ones who sold the girl into prostitution initially, so returning her to her home would merely give the family a chance to resell her. And even if a return to prostitution is not a danger, the girl, having spent time in prostitution, is often considered tainted, and so her family and neighbors may want nothing to do with her.[11]

While this was not true with all of the girls rescued in Sangli, most home situations are judged unsuitable and a rescued girl remains in the government remand home awaiting placement in a private rehabilitation home. During that time, ideally, NGO social workers visit the home to provide one-on-one counseling and in general to try to provide whatever is lacking in the care provided by the government. Real improvement often does not come until the girl is moved to a better aftercare facility.

Stage two: long-term aftercare facilities. A number of private organizations in India, many of them religious, have homes where they receive rescued girls and provide for their needs. There are too few of these facilities available, given the tremendous need, but the ones that exist generally do good work. Restore International does not yet have an aftercare facility of its own in India, but when possible, Restore staffers have facilitated the transfer of rescued girls to private homes where they can receive further counseling, job training, and education.

How successful is the rehabilitation that takes place in these facilities? In part, it depends on the age of the girl. The younger the girl, the greater the chance for successful rehabilitation. Girls twelve to fifteen years of age might be tenderhearted enough to respond well to the loving care they receive at rehabilitation homes. Older girls, sixteen or seventeen years old, often are more hardened by their suffering and find it nearly impossible to trust those who are trying to help them.

Once a girl turns eighteen, she is free to leave a rehabilitation home, hopefully taking advantage of the home's assistance in finding a job upon reentry into society. Until the day comes when she leaves, though, aftercare workers try to provide her with what she needs. Among these needs, one of the greatest is for medical care.

Repairing Damaged Health

Living in a brothel and being forced to take on multiple sexual partners daily exacts a terrible toll on a young girl's body. The brothel keepers often provide so little food, and food of such poor quality, that girls become malnourished and prone to illness. With what little money they are able to save for themselves, the girls may be able to buy some supplemental food, but then again, they may not. Meanwhile, they typically suffer from gynecological damage, sexually transmitted diseases, and viral or bacterial infections such as tuberculosis. The worst of their infections, of course, is HIV/AIDS—a death sentence for more than half of the sex workers in India.[12]

When they seek medical treatment, the girls often fall into the hands of corrupt doctors, who (like corrupt police officers) abdicate their professional responsibility to care for the girls and instead further exploit them. One journalist who investigated Mumbai's notorious Falkland Road red-light district reported, "Madams steer sick prostitutes to any one of the red-light area's 200 unlicensed doctors, who give them mood elevators, IV drips of colored water or medicinal herbs. Meanwhile, the debt-laden prostitutes pay for their 'treatment' with cash borrowed from mobbed-up moneylenders. And the mob collects a kickback from the quacks."[13]

Many of the girls are also pregnant or have small children. Given their other health problems and their young age, giving birth can be a hazardous experience for the girls. They need maternity care for themselves as well as pediatric care for their children.

All of this means that when girls are rescued they are usually in serious need of medical care. While they are in the hands of the government, they are (at least theoretically) able to access government-sponsored medical care, but the medical system in India is largely behind the times by Western standards and is terribly overburdened, and so the girls may not get the care they need. Those who wind up being placed in private rehabilitation homes often receive better medical attention. Of course, for those who are HIV positive, they are still under a death sentence, and they may not get life-extending drugs such as AZT that are more widely available in developed countries.

What should happen, among other things, is for social workers to encourage rescued girls to be tested for HIV and assist them in getting the best medical care they can. By getting placement in a private rehabilitation home, they can be put in a position where they are more likely to get good medical care. Helping a rescued girl get medical care from a private provider is what it often takes to see that she gets the treatment that she and her children (if any) need.

The medical complications of spending months or years in prostitution are bad enough, but added on top of them are emotional traumas. Rescued girls need specialized counseling.

Healing the Wounds of the Heart

Typically, a girl is either sold or abducted, then transported to a red-light district in an area where she may not even speak the language. Then she may be raped, beaten, and starved until she submits to prostituting herself.

She is used by men numerous times per day, every day, without a weekend break or vacation. She feels economically burdened because she is told over and over again that she owes her keeper a substantial amount of money to repay what was spent on her. She makes little or no money that she can spend on herself or send back home to her family. She prays that she won't get HIV, yet she knows that the lives of others in her profession are short. Imagine what all this must do to her spirit!

The Indian government provides only limited counseling for the rescued girls. In a survey of survivors of commercial sexual exploitation, only 44 percent said they had been given counseling while at a rescue home, and among these, most accorded the counseling service at best an average rating.[14] So our desire is to offer psychotherapy, whether individually or in a group setting, for the girls. It's not easy work, and there are no guarantees that a girl will ever return to a full measure of emotional health. Still, the counselors, knowing the importance of what they do, stick with the girls and often see progress being made. They have learned that the girls go through typical stages related to how long they have been out of the brothel.

Newly rescued girls. When girls are first rescued, they are usually angry and afraid. Their trauma is so deep that they are unable to trust anyone. Brainwashed by brothel keepers, they believe they still have a debt to pay to the brothel. Many wrestle with the feeling that they have let down their parents and will be unable to help them financially. Most are afraid of the future. They believe that prostitution is the only life for them. Once rescued, they wonder what good the future could possibly hold.

Sometimes girls go on hunger strikes for short periods of time, refuse to speak to counselors, or get hostile and abusive toward others. This is a fear reaction and is the first stage in their rehabilitation. These symptoms can last a week or much longer, depending on the girl.

One month after rescue. After the anger, fear, and confusion of the first few weeks in the remand home, things begin to get better. Although the government home is not a comfortable place and doesn't offer a lot of fun activities, the girls slowly begin to improve, thanks to the protection from abuse and rape. Girls become more willing to tell their story and are generally more cooperative with the counselors. The beginning signs of hope dawn in their faces.

Long-term rehabilitation. The greatest changes in attitude, emotions, and overall health are seen once the girls are transferred to long-term rehabilitation homes. Here they receive one-on-one and group counseling. Many homes have handicraft lessons, provide educational opportunities, and try to recreate the atmosphere of a loving home with firm discipline. Once the girls are surrounded by caring staff and are given healthy lifestyle alternatives, they begin to dream of their future, sometimes for the first time in years.

Maturity, healing, and recovery are a long process. After two years in a good rehabilitation home, many girls recover well and find joy and peace. They also begin to prepare for employment beyond the sex trade.

Ready to Support Herself

Women and girls in India, generally, are given fewer opportunities than males to go to school and learn marketable skills. Indeed, in India 90 percent of rural and 70 percent of urban women workers are unskilled.[15] Those girls who are forced into prostitution face even greater handicaps in this area. For example, devadasis have been dedicated to limited religious duties and prostitution from a young age. By the time girls are rescued from brothels, they are often illiterate, unskilled, and remarkably ignorant about the world. All they know is prostitution; what are they going to do when they are on their own?

Poverty was a large part of why a girl wound up in prostitution in the first place, so an important part of her rehabilitation must be equipping her to earn a living in another way. Rehabilitation facilities typically provide some remedial education and job training. Girls can learn to sew, do agricultural work, or find a job in a factory. The goal is to enable them to get a job, perhaps back within their home villages, and provide for themselves. They most likely will remain within the poorer classes of India, but at least they will be doing work that is safer and has dignity.

With education and vocational training, just as with housing, medical care, and counseling, Restore International's desire is to support and enhance the efforts of other government and private bodies. We do not yet have our own facility in India to provide aftercare for rescued girls, but that may one day change.

The Challenges and Opportunities of Aftercare

In Kampala, the capital city of Uganda, Restore International has already partnered in the operation of a home for rescued prostitutes from that central African country. Called the Rahab House, this facility offers the girls education, job training, counseling, and mentoring to break the cycle of trafficking and oppression. The young girls who live for a while at Rahab House have a wonderful opportunity to put a painful part of their past behind them and embark on a new and better life.

A part of Restore International's long-term plan for its work in India is to do much the same thing as we have done in partnering with the Rahab House. We envision establishing a therapeutic residential treatment facility that will provide a nurturing environment, loving and committed staff, job training, counseling, health care, and education. The goal will be to find each girl's particular gift and to support and encourage her to reach her potential. This will involve providing as many options as possible in microenterprise, the arts, and many other vocations.

We don't underestimate how hard the work will be. Indeed, in the aftercare work we have already undertaken, we have learned how difficult it can be to bring about change in the life of a girl who has been beaten down physically and emotionally. Rescued girls often don't expect things to change for the better for them—and sometimes don't even see the need to change. These girls often think they truly belong with the pimps and brothel keepers in the miserable life of prostitution, but with patience and perseverance, the bud of hope can be nurtured within them so that they can begin to see the possibility of a better life.

Many people in India are apathetic about ending child prostitution because they see it as just one more means of survival in a populous and poverty-stricken nation, but we can never give in to that mindset. Each girl rescued from a brothel is a special creation of God, unique and of infinite worth. She *deserves* a chance at a new life, and that is what we are determined to give. Aftercare completes the process of restoration for a girl who was tragically forced into prostitution as a slave.

Knowing what can be achieved with hard work and expertise, we are committed to continuing in—and expanding—our role in efforts to end the slavery of children and care for those who have been released.

TEN

From Here-Where?

The Future of Restore International

Restore International is committed to the great and beautiful nation of India and to her daughters trapped in prostitution slavery. Karishma is still being held captive in an Indian brothel (or so we fear), and so are hundreds of thousands of other young girls, and therefore our team will remain in India and do all we can to find these girls, get them out, and prosecute their exploiters. At the same time we realize that the problem of modern-day slavery goes far beyond the borders of India. And that means Restore is extending its reach around the globe as it seeks justice for exploited kids and the poorest of the poor.

Ours is a relatively new human rights organization, having been founded in 2004, but as this chapter explains, already we are expanding our work to child victimization hotspots in a number of countries. The problems we are seeking to address in each location we go to are terrible, and the potential for what we can accomplish is exciting, but as you read the stories of what we are doing and planning to do, perhaps you can reflect on just how much you might be able to do as you choose your passions. The important thing to remember is that we should be about action. It's the *do* component that is high on our agenda. And it is not *doing* so that we will be well regarded by others; it is *doing* because that's what we saw Jesus of Nazareth doing. I have observed that NGOs have a way of going into a new territory with a lot of enthusiasm and then somehow settling down, conducting business as usual, and losing their effectiveness. In contrast to that precedent, I'm not interested in Restore becoming merely *domiciled* in different countries; I'm interested in *doing* things for those who need our help where the strategic opportunities present themselves.

How much does a new Restore International center of operation really need? That's what I ask myself whenever we start a new work. And the answer I come up with is this: We need just a few capable and committed people and some basic supplies—a car, a phone, a medical plan, and so forth. We don't need a lot of equipment or fancy facilities; we don't need more computers or metal desks or office space. That all comes later. We just need to get about the work. This approach is non institutional, and it might sound naive, but I don't think it is reckless. Well, on second thought, maybe it *is* a bit reckless-but in an audacious way! The truth is, if I have to err, I want to err on the side of doing rather than of talking about doing. I don't want to get mired in setting up camp and getting comfortable and making everything just so before we act. Justice for exploited kids cannot wait for letterhead, decorating, and Web pages.

One of my colleagues who shares my passion for getting human rights work done is my friend Mohal, who runs a Restore program in India with a funny-sounding name.

Snekithar: You've Got a Friend in Tamil Nadu

Kumar was a bonded laborer working in the *beedi* (handmade cigarette) industry in India. He yearned for freedom and finally got it, but then he was faced with a problem: how would he support his family? He had a wife, Reeta Mary, who was prone to sickness, and four children in ages from infancy through the grade-school years. He and his wife were also taking care of two young relatives abandoned by their parents. Kumar tried to get work in the *beedi* industry as a paid daily laborer, but the factory owners refused to give him a job. He was then reduced to scavenging the woods for firewood and trying to sell it, averaging an income of less than fifty cents a day. Meanwhile, his family of eight lived in a shack thirty square feet in size.

That's when Snekithar stepped into his life. The term *snekithar* means "friend" in Tamil, and Snekithar is a project of Restore International in Tamil Nadu that befriends released bonded laborers like Kumar, as well as other socially and economically disadvantaged Indians.[1] It offers these poorly educated and largely unskilled persons basic vocational instruction and gives them employment producing handicrafts out of bamboo so that they can earn a living wage. The profits of this business are spent on starting other self-employment programs as well as supporting Christian educational ministries for children.

Kumar's family is one of thirty-five families currently being helped by this division of Restore International. While his income is small by Western standards, it is much better than what he was making by selling firewood. Through Snekithar, he is providing for his family and is even making plans to move them into a larger home. Most of all, he has now added dignity and hope to the freedom from slavery he had already won.

My friend Mohal is doing a great job at running Snekithar. In fact, Mohal has such a love for children, and such a proven ability at helping the needy, that I have asked him to set up new organizations to expand our services to India's needy kids. The intention is that these organizations will focus on finding and releasing bonded laborers and providing for the needs of the poorest of the poor in India. They will expand on the kinds of good works that Snekithar is already accomplishing. Mohal will know just how to make them do that.

Meanwhile, in other parts of the world, children are facing injustices that few of us have heard about and that fewer of us can comprehend once we've learned about them.

Restore International's Snekithar program for persons released from bonded labor teaches them to earn a labor through bamboo handicrafts.

Sacrifices to the Devil

"I was eight when I began to help out my ill father working on the surface of the mine in Chorolque," recalls former Bolivian miner Valentín Condori. "When he died, his co-workers let me into the pits to help carry the ore. Later I was digging rock, preparing dynamite charges and also setting them off. Thank God I never had an accident."

"We began in the early morning. We chewed coca leaf, smoked cigarettes, we drank a bit of alcohol, and that's how we got up the nerve to go into the mine."[2]

Condori's story is tragic, but far from rare. Although Bolivia has laws setting the minimum working age at fourteen and regulating dangerous labor environments, at least 13,500 children and adolescents are believed to be involved in tin, silver, and zinc mining in this poor South American nation. These children often lose their hearing from the noise of explosions and from heavy machinery, suffer lung damage by inhaling toxic gases and dust, and are exposed to accidents from handling explosives and from being crushed by rock. They rarely live past the age of forty, often dying from tuberculosis or silicosis brought on by contact with poisonous substances.[3]

The miners—children and grown-ups alike—fully realize the danger they face, and many of them deal with it in a surprising way. In a tradition going back to colonial times, the miners consider Tio, or Satan, to be their subterranean protector, and so the horned and red-eyed idols of Tio are found in every mine. After Sunday Mass in some places, miners gather for the sacrifice of a llama, whose blood they spread on themselves and splatter on the entrance to the mine to appease the supposed master of their underground workplace. This identification of Satan rather than God as holding sway in the mines is a telling comment on the conditions Bolivian miners face when working in the bowels of the earth.

The opportunity exists to rescue children from the hellish underworld of the Bolivian mines and give them lives of greater safety, health, and hope. No kids should be forgotten because they are in Tio's subterranean realm.

Restore International has been fortunate to have Jaime Aparicio on its team. He is an expert in international law and diplomacy and until recently served as Bolivia's ambassador to the United States. Ambassador Aparicio's intimate knowledge of the Bolivian and Latin American context, combined with his passion for protecting children, has made it possible for Restore International to find strategic ways to both be a part of the answer for Latin American teens and preteens and to participate in a meaningful way in other matters drawing upon Ambassador Aparicio's skills. For example, Ambassador Aparicio has been laboring extensively in Nicaragua to assist that country in its efforts for democracy. He is not only one of Restore's tremendous assets, but he has also been appointed chief of the Carter Center's mission to oversee elections in this Latin American country. Further, he introduced legislation for the Organization of American States.

The Tarnished Pearl of Africa

In 2004, Jan Egeland, UN under-secretary general for humanitarian affairs and emergency relief, stated in a news conference, "Northern Uganda to me remains the biggest neglected humanitarian emergency in the world." He was talking about a region of the world where for two decades fighting between a rebel army and government forces has overturned life for the population that calls that area home. Even more than usual in war-torn areas, the children have paid the price for the hatred in the hearts of their elders.

The rebel group, called the Lord's Resistance Army, is a ragtag force who claim to be rebels against the Ugandan army, but who have spent most of their time raiding defenseless villages, abducting children, and murdering, maiming, and torturing innocent civilians. The LRA is led by Joseph Kony, a self-proclaimed spirit medium who has used warped biblical interpretations to justify the horrifying violence he directed. Recent negotiations between the LRA and the government have improved the chances for peace in the region, but even the most hopeful scenario for the future must include a long period of recovery, due to the terrible violence carried out there.

Kony is a member of the Acholi tribe, which occupies much of northern Uganda. Early on he lost the support of his fellow Acholi (though many Acholi don't like the central Ugandan government either). And so, without volunteers coming in to swell the ranks of the insurgency, the LRA for years resorted to abducting children from rural areas of Acholiland, brainwashing them into believing the LRA was in the right, and putting guns in their hands to fight for their side—the victims becoming the victimizers. The LRA also abducted girls to act as sex slaves for Kony and the officers and men in his fighting force, as it did on the night of October 10, 1996, when two hundred LRA soldiers broke into St. Mary's College in Aboke and abducted 152 girls between the ages of thirteen and sixteen. In total, the LRA is believed to have kidnapped more than twenty thousand children, most of whom have died at the hands of the LRA or have died fighting for the LRA.

The tragedy of kids forced to become soldiers or the sex slaves of soldiers has been bad enough, but there has been another dimension of child victimization to the situation. For years, approximately twenty-five thousand boys and girls living in rural areas of Acholiland feared being stolen from their huts while they were sleeping, and so every evening they would walk (sometimes for miles) to the nearest town to spend the night in a public shelter, only to walk back again the morning. They are called "night commuters." Much of their childhood has been wasted in travel that is necessary solely to prevent them from losing their freedom.[4] With the prospect of peace in the region increasing, the number of night commuters has decreased dramatically, but the battle for these is kids far from over.

Upwards of two million Ugandans have moved into refugee camps in northern Uganda as a result of the fighting.[5] In fact, around 80 percent of the Acholi population became internally displaced persons (IDPs) living in the camps. The Ugandan military placed guards around these camps, but they have been inadequate to prevent LRA attacks designed to abduct new soldiers and force the displaced persons out of the camps and thus out of the government's sphere of influence. Meanwhile, life in the camps has been miserable. They are terribly crowded; there is too little food and water because at times aid workers have been ambushed by the LRA when trying to get in with supplies; HIV/AIDS is rampant; injustice prevails in the camps; and the IDPs have had a hard time telling whether it is more dangerous to stay in the camps or to leave them. The average age of the IDPs is in the low teens; many families are headed by children whose parents have died, leaving the responsibility for the siblings to them; and so a whole generation of Ugandans is growing up with nothing to do and few positive influences in their lives.

Who would want to go to such a lawless and violent environment as northern Uganda? People like you and I would! Why? Because that's where the need is. Our point person for Uganda, Ilea Dorsey, lives in the capital city of Kampala and is the embodiment of "do." The Ugandan government has eagerly welcomed our participation in a number of areas, since they are fully aware of the terrible conditions in the north, and we have already received requests to help in many areas. However fitful or smooth the path to peace in the north may be, Restore will be there to help improve life for the children and the poor. As with all things, we are executing our plans in a strategic manner.

In the fall of 2006 we coordinated with the chief justice of the Ugandan High Court to co-sponsor a conference for all the judges and justices of Uganda, which is upcoming. The purpose of the forum is to improve adjudication of cases where people require intervention by the courts to address human rights cases. This groundbreaking effort has had an impact on the entire national court system in Uganda and is as anticipated as it was well received.

Concurrent with the judicial conference, Restore International has gone on to partner with the justices in bringing to trial human rights cases that have been severely delayed in the northern city of Gulu due to rebel activity. These "Gulu sessions" are serving as a pilot project for other regions of the country. U.S.-based law students and attorneys are writing case briefs to assist with this initiative and are working hand in glove with the judges in Uganda to bring the rule of law back to this war-torn region.

In addition, Restore International is establishing secondary schools in the regions that have been ravaged by rebel activity in northern Uganda. These schools will train future leaders of the north and effect practical, tangible restoration in this devastated area.

Meanwhile, in the south, Restore International has joined in a three-way partnership with Rhema Ministries and Cornerstone Ministries to rescue minor girls from forced prostitution on the streets of the capital city, Kampala. Similar to our work with girls like Karishma in India, this effort in Uganda has been tremendously effective in identifying underage girls, pulling them out of their forced sexual labor, providing counseling and medical care, and (after an initial period of restoration in a group-home setting) enrolling them in a boarding school. This project is called the Rahab Project, and the home where the rescued girls live is called the Rahab House.

Uganda currently is Restore International's most active field of work. Along with the work we have done with the child prostitutes of India, we are laying the groundwork for expanded operations in other parts of the world where children and the poorest of the poor lack the justice they deserve.

Serious Fun

Starting in offices over a Laundromat, Restore International has found many opportunities truly to serve in various countries. Who knows where we might go next? Our compass is to do those things Jesus of Nazareth was doing and bring as many people along as want to go! One thing is certain: while keeping our office over the Laundromat, we will continue looking for the worst injustices practiced upon the world's children and try to figure out what we can do to make a positive difference in their lives. We have no illusions that this will be easy or that we are something special, but we do know that we are ready to show up. We expect some failures along with our successes. We know that we are up against powerful interests and are working in places where cultural and political forces that we may not fully understand can easily cloud an issue and impede our efforts. However, from our experiences in India, Uganda, and elsewhere, we know that, as we sign up dedicated and capable people, adopt best practices, and pour on determination, toughness, and persistence, we can see amazing successes on behalf of children.

When an Indian youth is no longer sold as a slave, we will have made a dent.

When that same Indian has a good-paying job and something to do in the marketplace, we will have made a contribution.

When a young Ugandan girl is pulled out of the brothel where she serves customers against her will, we will have made a difference.

When a Ugandan teenager is able to go back to her village free from the fear of being attacked or kidnapped, we will have succeeded in part.

Toughness and persistence can indeed accomplish much. And beyond that, I'm naive enough to believe that creativity, love, and even fun can be a part of this work. Yes, fun. I have a confession to make: I *enjoy* my work with Restore International. And so do the other people who work alongside me. It is true that the issues we work on are serious, grim, and even revolting, and sometimes I just have to take a break from talking about the subjects presented. But, then again, sometimes—believe it or not—the work seems to not to be work at all because it just feels so good to be spending our days bringing justice to children around the world who are about the ages our my own kids.

We are also keen on "doing life" with people, not doing commerce. Even when I am promoting Restore International's work to a group of potential supporters we rarely ask for money; rather than doing fund-raising, we want to engage people. As a result, we just tell the story and let people decide on their own the way in which they might want to get involved.

Anyone can make a difference in justice problems around the world, such as child exploitation. Anyone—that includes *you*.

PART THREE:

The End of Slavery

ELEVEN
Toward a Modern Abolition Movement

What You Can Do to End Slavery Now

William Wilberforce was born into a prosperous merchant family in Kingston upon Hull, a North Sea port of England, in 1759. During his childhood, relatives took him to an evangelical Anglican church, where he came to revere a guest preacher called John Newton, a former slave ship captain who went on to write the still-popular song "Amazing Grace." During his years at Cambridge University, and in the early years after his election to Parliament at age twenty-one, Wilberforce led a dissipated life. Not until 1785, when he read a devotional book by Philip Doddridge, did he personally embrace Christian faith and begin living his life with more serious purposes in mind. Following a conversation with Prime Minister William Pitt under a tree at Croydon, where they discussed the slave trade and abolition, Wilberforce took up the cause that would mark his life until its end.

Wilberforce became the parliamentary leader of the abolition movement in England in 1787, and two years later he introduced the Abolition Bill to the House of Commons for the first time with a speech considered to be one of the most eloquent ever delivered before that body. Opponents of the bill, however, successfully used delaying tactics to prevent its being voted upon. Once more, in 1792, Wilberforce delivered a renowned speech upon the evils of the slave trade in support of his bill, but the amendment of the bill to add the word "gradual" gave slavery's supporters a chance to postpone the ending of the slave trade for several more years. Finally, in

1807, after years of speaking and writing by Wilberforce, Thomas Clarkson, and other British abolitionists, Parliament passed a bill outlawing the slave trade by British maritime interests. On the occasion, the House of Commons gave Wilberforce three cheers—a rare honor in a body where applause is forbidden.

Although the trade in slaves became illegal in 1807, slavery still existed in British colonies, and indeed there was little political will at the time for total emancipation. In 1812 Wilberforce started work on the Slave Registration Bill, reasoning that if slaves were registered, it could be proved whether they had been recently transported from Africa in violation of the new law. Passage of this bill failed, however, and by 1815, instead of backing down from his cause, Wilberforce became bolder by arguing openly for the emancipation of slaves. Wilberforce's health began failing, but he continued attacking slavery at public meetings as well as in the House of Commons and wrote pamphlets on the subject. He resigned from the House of Commons in 1825, and his last public appearance was at a meeting of the Anti-Slavery Society in 1830. Meanwhile, the Emancipation Bill was gaining support in Parliament, and its last commons reading before passage occurred on July 26, 1833, including its provision to financially compensate the owners of freed slaves. On hearing the news, Wilberforce declared, "Thank God that I have lived to witness a day in which England is willing to give twenty millions sterling for the abolition of slavery." Three days later he died.

The Possibility of Ending Slavery

The cause for which Wilberforce and other dedicated abolitionists fought is not over, despite the universal outlawing of slavery. Indeed, the Anti-Slavery Society, of which Wilberforce was a member, still exists today because slavery still exists today.[1] There are, in fact, more people on the earth right now enduring slavery and slavery-like conditions than there were in 1833 when William Wilberforce died. The conclusion is obvious, therefore: we need a new abolition movement to complete the work, ending slavery in fact as well as in law.

Can slavery really be ended? Might not its continued existence in our day mean that it is an intractable problem, no more possible to eliminate from the human race than we can eliminate disease from the human body?

From one perspective, modern-day slavery does not seem like such a fearsome foe to defeat. While slavery has proved stubborn and adaptive, it is not the cultural or economic force it once was, and this means the cost of eliminating it is not so high as it could be. Consider this historical precedent: In the American South prior to the Civil War, slavery had become a way of life and the basis for much of the economy in what would become the Confederate states. When the Yankee abolitionists called for an end to slavery, then, they were threatening the very basis of the culture for an entire region of the Union. That is not at all the case in the modern abolition movement. No nation on the face of the earth today is so invested in slavery that the removal of the practice from within its borders would threaten the continuation of the nation or even the continuation of its present regime. In our day, then, ending slavery is not necessarily so daunting a prospect as, say, ending militant Islamic terrorism or disarming rogue nations possessing nukes. We can do this, if the will is there.

Illegal slavery has gone into hiding, where it survives by staying undercover, but public attention, international cooperation in anti-trafficking efforts, and the application of modern information technologies can help to drive it out into the light of day, where it can be destroyed. There is some evidence that traffickers in some places are making use of new technologies, such as European traffickers who use encryption software in coordinating the importation of underage prostitutes from the East. But, by and large, slavery today exists in more primitive areas of the world where the social system is inadequate. As nations develop, becoming more democratic, more prosperous, and more open, the likelihood is that slavery may begin to shrink in real numbers just as it has shrunk as a percentage of the world population. In the meantime, the International Justice Mission, Restore International, and other fine organizations play an important role by keeping the issue before an information-overloaded public and especially by attacking slavery head-on where it lives. In this way, bit by bit, the light defeats the darkness.

I agree with social researcher Kevin Bales when he states, "Human beings may always find new ways to enslave others, but I believe there is reason for optimism in the fight against slavery. This is the first generation to have developed a general consensus against slavery, and the first generation that has the opportunity to develop global mechanisms to root out and eradicate slavery. It may be that slavery can never be permanently eradicated, but, like many infectious diseases, it might be generally suppressed and watchfully controlled as new forms emerge. Such mechanisms would be one of the best imaginable legacies of our generation."[2]

With the encouragement of abolitionists William Wilberforce and Thomas Clarkson, Josiah Wedgwood in 1787 had a medallion created showing a black slave with the motto "Am I not a man and a brother?" In the same way, Restore International seeks innovative ways to publicize the proble of modern-day slavery.

How to End Slavery

There is no quick or easy to solution to the problem of modern-day slavery. Just as slavery exists in diverse forms in many places today, so it must be fought all over and in all sorts of ways. The modern abolition movement, then, is the coming together of international bodies, regional cooperatives, nation-states, nongovernmental organizations, and individuals to offer whatever power and expertise they have to the fight against slavery. Restore International is not only a part of this coalition, but also works for the building of this movement by presenting over and over again, in whatever forum and form it can, the need for all to take notice of modern-day slavery and do something about it.

Abolition work goes on at all levels. As we know, slavery has been illegal around the world for some time now, yet many national and international bodies are still trying to improve their laws, policies, and protocols to tighten the strictures placed upon slavery and slavery-like practices.[3] In some cases, this is necessary because there were loopholes in the legal wording. In other cases, it is necessary because slavery itself is changing and so demands a new legal and political response. Most of this work is to the good, though in my opinion it is far from being enough to end slavery on its own. What we need more than better laws is better enforcement of the laws.

It is at lower levels, and on a smaller scale, that the most effective anti-trafficking work can be accomplished, I believe. Here is where non-governmental organizations, community-based organizations, faith-based organizations, and even for-profit corporations can contribute. Trafficking is usually carried out by relatively small networks of evil-minded people, so small networks of right-minded people are needed to combat them. At this level, groups of modern-day abolitionists can bring legal instruments to bear on traffickers they identify and find ways to make unprofitable what is, after all, an economic system.[4]

And then there is the most intimate level of involvement with the issue of all: the level of the individual. William Wilberforce has shown that individuals can make a difference in the fight against slavery. The nineteenth century or the twenty-first—it doesn't matter: each one of us, if we care enough and are willing to act, can make a difference in the war on slavery. That's what I discovered when this "recovering lawyer" vowed to spend the rest of his life working for real justice worldwide, not just the trading of dollars in U.S. courtrooms. The truth is, practical actions are at hand for each of us to join in the modern abolition movement.

Consider these action steps you can take.

• *Stay informed.* Reading this book can be just the beginning of your education on modern-day slavery. Learn more about this global problem or about a particular type of it (such as the commercial sexual exploitation of children) that concerns you the most. How? Here are some ideas: Search the catalog of your public library for more books on the subject. Subscribe to a Google alert so that you will be informed of the latest articles on a subject related to modern-day slavery.[5] Bookmark the Restore International Web site and put your name on our mailing list to receive updates about our work.[6]

• *Spread the word.* As you learn more about modern-day slavery, share that information with the people in your life. This could range from talking it over with your friends and family to speaking publicly before a church or community group. The more people who know about the problem, the more likely we all are to get something done about it.

• *Be careful what you buy.* I don't advise that you boycott slave-possessing nations across the board. After all, when you buy products from a reputable company operating in a poor nation, you are actually improving the nation's economic environment and indirectly reducing the demand for slaves. When you hear a reliable report that a particular company uses slave or child labor, then buy from a competitor of that company even if it means you must spend a little extra money. And then, when you get home, write to the offending company to explain why you have chosen not to buy its products.

• *Write to your elected officials.* When you have a concern about human trafficking, or when an anti-trafficking bill is coming up in Congress, respectfully write to the appropriate legislator to express your view.[7]

• *Consider working for Restore International.* Restore is growing and needs dedicated, qualified employees for a number of roles within the organization. If you have the appropriate skills, consider applying for one of the jobs. You could be working on the frontlines of the new abolition movement.[8]

• *Sign up for a Restore International vision trip.* Periodically, Restore International schedules vision trips to provide opportunities for interested individuals to experience the impact of Restore International firsthand. The purpose of the vision trip is to give participants a permanently enriched and changed understanding of confronting injustice and rebuilding lives. Join or organize a vision trip to India, Uganda, or one of our other areas of operation.[9]

• *Book a Restore International speaker.* I love to speak to groups about justice work and so do others at Restore International. If you would like us to address your group, write or call with your request.[10]

• *Contribute financially.* Restore International is funded by a combination of public grants and private donations. We cannot continue to do our work, much less expand, without adequate financial backing. So if you are concerned about worldwide slavery and want to do something to stop it, invest in an organization that is action oriented.[11]

• *Pray.* If you are a person of faith, as I am, pray for Karishma and her sisters and brothers around the world who are trapped in servitude for others. Slavery is an attack upon the spirit; to me, it seems appropriate for us to call on spiritual power to come against it.

Whether or not you choose to be involved in the work of Restore International, I urge you to find your own audacious ways to help solve the problems faced by children, the poor, and other needy people. Jesus of Nazareth showed us the importance of caring about others and acting in faith and boldness. The world has not yet fully seen what can be accomplished when individuals like you and me will put aside our fears and hesitations and go all out, with love in our hearts, to serve others.

EPILOGUE

The miracle each of us has longed for has happened! You are going to love this! Remember how we discussed the importance of "the one?" Karishma, whose name means "miracle," was found as this manuscript was being completed.

Restore International operatives first discovered this girl of around twelve years of age in the brothel district of Miraj, India, on October 18, 2005 (see chapter one). She was whisked away by traffickers before police raided her brothel, and then all our leads ran out and our attempts to find her became fruitless. On May 6, 2006, just as I was doing the revisions on the manuscript for this book, Karishma was discovered in another brothel located in a nearby city.

It happened this way.

Informants in the Sangli-Miraj area put the founder of Freedom Firm—another excellent human rights organization working in India—together with Karishma's brother, Satish. (Somehow it had never come out before that Karishma even had a brother.) Satish said that Karishma was living in the slum area of Sadar Bazaar in Kolhapur, thirty-seven miles away from Miraj, though he could not provide a specific address where she could be found.

This lack of specificity was a serious problem, because Sadar Bazaar is a vast area, housing thousands of people, but the human rights worker did what he could anyway. First, he made some quick surveys of the Sadar Bazaar red-light areas. When this failed to turn up any sign of Karishma, he went to the local police and asked for help.

A Kolhapur police superintendent, Suraj More, took the scanty information that the justice workers could provide, including a photo of Karishma, and instructed his men to find the girl. Some of the police officers, in turn, called in one of their regular informants, who recognized Karishma from the photo and said that he knew where she was living. By this time, excitement was running high among the justice workers and Karishma's brother.

That very day, the police informant led the group to a brothel on the edge of town. The police officers raided the place, and Karishma was spotted running out the back door. Undoubtedly, like other trafficked prostitutes, she had been taught that she belonged to her keeper and that the police were her enemies. As she ran out the door, she saw nothing but open fields before her and realized that she could not get away from the officers. So she turned around, walked back to the brothel, and submitted to being taken into custody.

In the days that followed, a legal case was filed, the brothel keeper was arrested, and Karishma was remanded to a government home for children. Karishma is safe at last. In the months and years to come, Karishma, like other rescued prostitution victims, will need to undergo extensive aftercare to ensure that she can step into a healthy future. It won't be easy. She won't quickly learn to trust others, to believe that she is a person whose value goes beyond what her body is worth to perverts, nor to hope for a future including productive labor and perhaps a family. At least now she is free, with the shining possibility before her of living a good life in the liberty that should have been hers all along.

My heart soars with the knowledge that I'm now living in a world where Karishma is free, and so I add this epilogue with joy. Of course I haven't forgotten that millions of other children and adults are still trapped in slave conditions, and I am just as committed to doing everything I can to help them, but today I take the opportunity to savor the freedom of this one young girl. She's the "one" we have considered in this book; she has infinite value to her Creator; and she's worth everything it has taken to pull her out of the clutches of her slave owners.

Welcome back, Karishma!

APPENDIX
Legal Instruments Related to Modern-Day Slavery

(Especially the Forced Prostitution of Children in India)

International Human Rights Instruments
- The United Nations Charter[1]
- The Universal Declaration of Human Rights
- The International Covenant on Civil and Political Rights
- The International Covenant on Economic, Social and Cultural Rights
- The Convention against Torture and other Cruel, Inhuman or Degrading Treatment or Punishment
- Principles and Guidelines on Human Rights and Human Trafficking

International Instruments against Slavery and Practices Similar to Slavery
- The League of Nations Slavery Convention of 1926
- The Supplementary Convention on the Abolition of Slavery, the Slave Trade and Institutions and Practices Similar to Slavery of 1956

International Trafficking Instruments
- The United Nations Millennium Declaration
- Convention for the Suppression of the Traffic in Persons and of the Exploitation of the Prostitution of Others

- The United Nations Convention against Transnational Organized Crime
- The Protocol to Prevent, Suppress and Punish Trafficking in Persons, Especially Women and Children (Supplementing the United Nations Convention against Transnational Organized Crime)
- The Recommended Principles and Guidelines on Human Rights and Human Trafficking

Asian Regional Trafficking Instruments
- The Bangkok Accord and Plan of Action to Combat Trafficking in Women (the Bangkok Accord)
- The ARIAT Regional Action Plan
- The ASEM Action Plan to Combat Trafficking in Persons, Especially Women and Children (the ASEM Action Plan)
- The SAARC Convention on Preventing and Combating Trafficking in Women and Children for Prostitution (the SAARC Convention)
- The Co-Chair's Statement from the Bali Ministerial Conference on People Smuggling, Trafficking in Persons and Related Transnational Crime (the Bali Conference Co-Chair's Statement)

International and Asian Regional Migration Instruments
- The International Convention on the Protection of the Rights of all Migrant Workers and Members of their Families
- The Bangkok Declaration on Irregular Migration

International Labor Instruments
- ILO Forced Labor Convention No. 29 of 1930 and Forced Labor (Regulation) Recommendation No. 36 of 1930
- ILO Abolition of Forced Labor Convention No. 105 of 1957
- ILO Protection of Wages Convention No. 95 of 1949 and Protection of Wages Recommendation No. 85 of 1949
- ILO Minimum Wage Fixing Convention No. 131 of 1970 and Minimum Wage Fixing Recommendation No. 135 of 1970
- ILO Employment Service Convention No. 88 of 1948 and Employment Service Recommendation No. 83 of 1948
- ILO Equal Remuneration Convention No. 100 of 1951 and Equal Remuneration Recommendation 90 of 1951
- ILO Discrimination (Employment and Occupation) Convention No. 111 of 1958 and Discrimination (Employment and Occupation) Recommendation No. 111 of 1958

- ILO Private Employment Agencies Convention No. 181 of 1997 and Private Employment Agencies Recommendation No. 188 of 1997

International and Asian Regional Gender-Specific Instruments
- The Convention on the Elimination of All Forms of Discrimination against Women
- The Declaration on the Elimination of Violence against Women
- The Beijing Declaration and Platform for Action
- The Jakarta Declaration and Plan of Action for the Advancement of Women in Asia and the Pacific

International and Asian Regional Child-Specific Instruments
- The Convention on the Rights of the Child
- The Optional Protocol to the CRC on the Sale of Children, Child Prostitution and Child Pornography
- ILO Minimum Age for Admission to Employment Convention No. 138
- ILO Worst Forms of Child Labor Convention No. 182 and ILO Worst Forms of Child Labor Recommendation No. 190
- Programme of Action for the Prevention of the Sale of Children, Child Prostitution and Child Pornography
- Programme of Action for the Elimination of the Exploitation of Child Labor
- The SAARC Convention on Regional Arrangements for the Promotion of Child Welfare in South Asia

United States Instruments
- The Trafficking Victims Protection Act
- The Trafficking Victims Protection Reauthorization Act
- The PROTECT Act (Prosecutorial Remedies and Other Tools to end Exploitation of Children Today Act)

Indian Instruments
- The Immoral Trafficking (Prevention) Act
- The Bonded Labor System (Abolition) Act
- The Juvenile Justice (Care and Protection of Children) Act
- The Child Labor (Prohibition and Regulation) Act
- Karnataka Devadasis (Prohibition of Dedication) Bill
- Maharasthra Protection of Commercial Sex Workers Act

NOTES

Preface

    1. Kevin Bales, *Disposable People: New Slavery in the Global Economy* (Berkeley: University of California Press, 1999), 9.

    2. Ibid., 7.

Chapter 1: The One Who Got Away

    1. The day after we arrived in Sangli, we were to told that the police had arranged a meeting of brothel owners in that city and had advised them on how to avoid being caught by us. This goes to show the level of collusion between police and red-light district traffickers in this part of India.

    2. A major government-sponsored study into the trafficking of women and children in India states the following:

"Children of women who are subjected to CSE [commercial sexual exploitation] are extremely vulnerable to being trafficked into CSE. The research by WISE shows that a large number of children of 'sex workers' are, in fact, trafficked into sexual exploitation. The vulnerability is the highest in this group of children because:

- most of these children are born out of 'illegitimate' relationships,
- the parents themselves abet trafficking, mostly for commercial gain,
- they lack care and attention,

- they lack education and opportunities to grow and develop,
- they are deprived of livelihood options, and
- they are denied their basic rights such as the right to live, right to freedom, right against exploitation and right to legal redressal of grievances.

"One comes across many such cases where the child is given away to another 'sex worker' (mostly aged ones) for 'adoption' or 'to be looked after.' There is always a price involved in such surrogate parenting. Beyond a point, these foster mothers do not take care of the children and they traffic them into CSE at the first opportunity. Similarly, when a victim affected by AIDS dies and leaves her children to the care of nobody in particular or another victim, they become easy targets of exploitation" ("Children in Brothels: Extremely Vulnerable to Trafficking and Sexual Exploitation," in Sankar Sen, ed., *Trafficking in Women and Children in India* [New Delhi: Orient Longman, 2005], 540).

3. Matthew 18:14, New International Version.

Chapter 2: For Sale: Human Beings

1. Kevin Bales, *Disposable People: New Slavery in the Global Economy* (Berkeley: University of California Press, 1999), 9. Bales estimates a total of 27 million slaves in the world, so by his reckoning, the 15 to 20 million bonded laborers in the subcontinental region make up more than half the total.

2. India's Bonded Labour System (Abolition) Act of 1976, as its name suggests, specifically outlaws this form of slavery. Accessed online at www.helplinelaw.com/bareact/index.

3. Mudalali is pronounced MOO-duh-LAY-lee.

4. It's a common misconception that the term trafficking applies only to the transportation of persons across national borders. Actually, as the U.S. State Department says, the term "denotes the act of placing someone in servitude and everything done knowingly that surrounds or contributes to it" (U.S. State Department, Office to Monitor and Combat Trafficking in Persons, "Trafficking in Persons Report," June 2005, 10; accessed online at www.state.gov/documents/organization/47255.pdf).

5. Among recent institutional definitions of slavery or slavery-like conditions are the following: The Rome Final Act of 1998, which established the International Criminal Court, defines enslavement as "the exercise of any or all of the powers attaching to the right of ownership over a person and includes the exercise of such power in the course of trafficking in persons, in

particular women and children" (Rome Statute of the International Criminal Court, 1988, article 7[2]c; accessed online at www.un.org/law/icc/statute/romefra.htm). The United Nations Protocol to Prevent, Suppress and Punish Trafficking in Persons, especially Women and Children (2000), defines trafficking in persons as "the recruitment, transportation, transfer, harboring or receipt of persons, by means of threat or use of force or other forms of coercion, of abduction, of fraud, of deception, of the abuse of power or of a position of vulnerability or of the giving or receiving of payments or benefits to achieve the consent of a person having control over another person, for the purpose of exploitation. Exploitation shall include, at a minimum, the exploitation of the prostitution of others or other forms of sexual exploitation, forced labor or services, slavery or practices similar to slavery, servitude or the removal of organs" (Protocol to Prevent, Suppress and Punish Trafficking in Persons Especially Women and Children, supplementing the United Nations Convention against Transnational Organized Crime, 2000, article 3[a]; accessed online at www.ohchr.org/english/law/protocoltraffic.htm). The U.S. Trafficking Victims Protection Act of 2000 defines "severe forms of trafficking" as "(a) sex trafficking in which a commercial sex act is induced by force, fraud, or coercion, or in which the person induced to perform such an act has not attained 18 years of age; or (b) the recruitment, harboring, transportation, provision, or obtaining of a person for labor or services, through the use of force, fraud, or coercion for the purpose of subjection to involuntary servitude, peonage, debt bondage, or slavery" (Victims of Trafficking and Violence Protection Act, 2000, sect. 103 [7(b)]; accessed online at www.state.gov/documents/organization/10492.pdf). The International Labor Organization, in its original convention on the subject, the Forced Labour Convention, defines forced labor as "all work or service which is exacted from any person under the menace of any penalty and for which the said person has not offered himself voluntarily" (Forced Labour Convention, 1930, article 2[1]). The other fundamental ILO instrument, the Abolition of Forced Labour Convention, specifies that forced labor can never be used for the purpose of economic development or as a means of political education, discrimination, labor discipline, or punishment for having participated in strikes (Abolition of Forced Labour Convention, 1957, article 1). Both definitions are reaffirmed in the ILO's 2005 report called, "A Global Alliance against Forced Labour: Global Report under the Follow-up to the ILO Declaration on Fundamental Principles and Rights at Work," accessed online at www.ilo.org/public/english/publication.ht,

6. Kevin Bales, *Understanding Global Slavery: A Reader* (Berkeley: University of California Press, 2005), 57.

7. International Labour Office, "Global Alliance," 10. From the ILO perspective, slavery is only one type of forced labor.

8. U.S. State Department, Office to Monitor and Combat Trafficking in Persons, "Trafficking in Persons Report," June 2006, 6; accessed online at www.state.gov/documents/organization/66086.pdf.

9. Bales, *Disposable People*, 9; Bales, *Understanding Global Slavery*, 6.

10. Bales, *Understanding Global Slavery*, 88–89.

11. Ibid., 8.

12. Office to Monitor and Combat Trafficking in Persons, "Trafficking in Persons Report," June 2005, 10, slightly adapted.

13. Undoubtedly the practice of slavery predated laws permitting and regulating it.

14. See the appendix for more legal instruments relating to modern-day slavery.

15. Bales, *Disposable People*, 5.

16. David Brion Davis, "Introduction: The Problem of Slavery," in *A Historical Guide to World Slavery*, eds., Seymour Drescher and Stanley L. Engerman (New York: Oxford University Press, 1998), ix.

17. Office to Monitor and Combat Trafficking in Persons, "Trafficking in Persons Report," June 2005, 6.

18. International Labour Organization, "Global Alliance," 15.

19. Quoted in Bales, *Understanding Global Slavery*, 33.

20. Francis T. Miko, Congressional Research Service, "Trafficking in Women and Children: The U.S. and International Response," updated March 26, 2004, 7; accessed online at www.fpc.state.gov/documents/organization/31990.pdf. Other estimates, however, put the number as high as fifty thousand. See Women's Bureau of the U.S. Department of Labor, "Trafficking in Persons: A Guide for Non-Governmental Organizations," 2002, 2; accessed online at www.justice.gov/crt/crim/wetf/trafficbrochure.pdf.

21. Bales, *Disposable People*, 9.

22. Bales, *Understanding Global Slavery*, appendix 2.

23. Office to Monitor and Combat Trafficking in Persons, "Trafficking in Persons Report," June 2005, 28.

24. Office to Monitor and Combat Trafficking in Persons, "Trafficking in Persons: Country Reassessment," September 22, 2005. Accessed online at www.state.gov/g/tip/rls/other/53913.htm.

25. Office to Monitor and Combat Trafficking in Persons, "Trafficking in Persons Report," June 2006, 46.

26. Office to Monitor and Combat Trafficking in Persons, "Trafficking in Persons Report," 13–14.

27. Asian Development Bank, "Combating Trafficking of Women and Children in South Asia: Regional Synthesis Paper for Bangladesh, India, and Nepal," April 2003, 8. Accessed online at www.adb.org/Documents/ Books/Combating_Trafficking/default.asp.

28. Bales, *Understanding Global Slavery*, 155.

29. HumanTrafficking.com, "Human Trafficking 101: Who Are the Traffickers?" Accessed online at www.humantrafficking.com/ humantrafficking/trafficking_ht3/who_traffickers.htm.

30. Thanh-Dam Truong, "Organised Crime and Human Trafficking." Accessed online at www.ahrchk.net/news.

31. International Labour Organization, *International Programme on the Elimination of Child Labour,* "Every Child Counts: New Global Estimates on Child Labour," 2002; accessed online at www.ilo.org/public/ english/publication.htm See also International Labour Organization, International Programme on the Elimination of Child Labour, "Unbearable to the Human Heart: Child Trafficking and Action to Eliminate It," 2002; accessed online at www.ilo.org/public/english/standards/ipec/publ/childtraf/ unbearable.pdf.

32. UNICEF, "The State of the World's Children 2006: Excluded and Invisible," 2006, 49. Accessed online at www.unicef.org/sowc06/pdfs/ sowc06_fullreport.pdf.

33. Office to Monitor and Combat Trafficking in Persons, "Trafficking in Persons Report," 5, slightly adapted.

34. Much of the following material in this section of the chapter is based upon the State Department's "Trafficking in Persons Report," 12–15.

35. Office to Monitor and Combat Trafficking in Persons, "Trafficking in Persons Report," 6, slightly adapted.

36. Si Johnston, "Protest 4," EmergingChurch.info, slightly adapted. Accessed online at www.emergingchurch.info/events/protest4.htm.

Chapter 3: Rape for Profit

1. Specifically, the population was 1,028,700,000 (Census of India, accessed online at www.censusindia.net/results/population.html).

2. U.S. State Department, Bureau of Democracy, Human Rights, and Labor, "Country Reports on Human Rights Practices, 2004: India" (released February 25, 2005). Accessed online at www.state.gov/g/drl/rls/hrrpt/2004/41740.htm. Other estimates for the total number of prostitutes in India range higher and lower than the State Department figure. For example, the Indian Association for the Rescue of Fallen Women estimated in 1992 that India had 15.5 million prostitutes (Sankar Sen, ed., *Trafficking in Women and Children in India* [New Delhi: Orient Longman, 2005], 13; accessed online at www.ashanet.org/focusgroups/sanctuary/articles/ReportonTrafficking.pdf). Some sources also put the total number of child prostitutes worldwide at a much higher figure. The British medical journal Lancet, for example, said the true number may be as high as 10 million (cited in Nicholas D. Kristof, "Slavery in Our Time," *The New York Times*, January 22, 2006; accessed online at www.aegis.com/news/nyt/2006/NYT060108.html).

3. Robert I. Friedman, "India's Shame: Sexual Slavery and Political Corruption Are Leading to an AIDS Catastrophe," *The Nation*, April 8, 1996, 12.

4. "SAARC: CS Groups Demand Implementation of SAARC Convention on Human Trafficking," *Pakistan Newswire*, January 2, 2004; cited in The Protection Project, "India." Accessed online at www.protectionproject.org/.

5. "UN Maps Human Trafficking," *Associated Press*, May 14, 2003; cited in Protection Project.

6. Sen, 12. See also Human Rights Watch/Asia, "Rape for Profit: Trafficking of Nepali Women and Girls to India's Brothels," 1995; accessed online at www.hrw.org/reports/pdfs/c/crd/india957.pdf.

7. Friedman, 11–12.

8. Ibid., 14.

9. Protection Project.

10. Quoted in Sen, 518.

11. "A Study of Brothels and Their Earnings in Mumbai, Pune and Surat," in Sen, 569–70.

12. This amount in U.S. dollars, as elsewhere in this book, has been calculated according to the early 2006 rate of exchange.

13. Joseph Ganthia, *Child Prostitution in India* (New Delhi: Concept, 1999), 20; cited in Sen, 14.

14. G. R. Gupta, unpublished report "Review of Literature for ARTWAC" (New Delhi: Institute of Social Sciences, 2003); cited in Sen, 18.

15. An Indian NGO called SANLAAP addressed the issue of recategorizing sex trafficking as sex work: "The simple but inevitable questions that came in our minds were as follows:

"a. When it starts with violence & sexual abuse how can we call it 'work'?

"b. When power relations are unequal and exploitative how can we call it work?

"c. When men and some women earn from selling a child's body, a human being, how can we call it work?

"d. An action that violates human rights, how can we call it work?

"e. If female genital mutilation have been rejected by women groups, why would wouldn't we reject rape of a girl child which is the basis and beginning of prostitution? How can we call this work?

"f. Purchase and sale of girls, through threats, trickery, deceit and false promises are the ways through which girls and young women are trafficked and forced into prostitution. Do we call it work?" (SANLAAP, "Human Rights and Sex Trafficking," October 12, 1999; accessed online at www3.undp.org/ww/women-health1/msg00123.html).

16. Yauvani (not her real name) was rescued from a Sangli, India, brothel in a Restore International–instigated rescue operation on May 20, 2005. This information comes from a post-rescue interview with Restore International personnel.

17. Alison Phinney, *Trafficking of Women and Children for Sexual Exploitation in the Americas* (Washington, D.C.: Inter-American Commission of Women, 2001); quoted in Sen, 9.

18. Sen, chapter 9.

19. Friedman, 16–19.

20. Sen, 121.

21. Twenty percent of respondents to a survey admitted to trafficking their own relatives. Since the survey was completely voluntary (that is, the traffickers could hide the truth if they wanted), the true percentage may have been much higher. Of those who admitted to trafficking relatives, three-quarters said the victims were under the age of eighteen at the time of trafficking (Sen, 122).

22. Quoted in ibid., 519.

23. Ibid., 120–21.

24. Ibid., chapter 14.

25. Ibid., 122.

26. S. R. Rozario et al., *Trafficking in Women and Children in India* (New Delhi: Uppal, 1988); cited in Sen, 12. In a large survey, women and girls rescued from brothels were asked about their treatment during transit. According to their responses, 19.3 percent had been physically abused, 33.5 percent had been sexually abused, 11.7 percent had been verbally abused, and 35.5 percent had been victims of multiple abuses, including drugging, death threats, and deprivation (Sen, 77).

27. Nirmala Niketan, unpublished report "Review of Literature for ARTWAC: Maharashtra" (Mumbai: Nirmala Niketan College of Social Work, 2003); quoted in Sen, 12.

28. Quoted in Soma Wadhwa, "For Sale: Childhood," *Outlook India*, February 23, 1998. Accessed online at www.outlookindia.com/full.

29. Sen, chapter 8.

30. Ibid., 105.

31. Ibid., chapter 7.

32. Ibid., 99.

33. One hundred rupees was equal to about $2.25 in U.S. currency at the early 2006 exchange rate.

34. Sen, 87.

35. Anahita (not her real name) was rescued from a Sangli, India, brothel in a Restore International–instigated rescue operation on May 20, 2005. This information comes from a post-rescue interview with Restore International personnel.

36. Asian Development Bank, "Combating Trafficking of Women and Children in South Asia: Regional Synthesis Paper for Bangladesh, India, and Nepal," April 2003, 45. Accessed online at www.adb.org/Documents/ Books/Combating_Trafficking/default.asp.

37. Ibid., 48.

38. Ibid., 49.

39. See especially articles 15 through 17 of the Indian Constitution. Accessed online at www.lawmin.nic.in/coi.htm.

40. The Web site *Indian Child* explains the caste system like this: "Castes are ranked, named, endogamous (in-marrying) groups, membership in which is achieved by birth. There are thousands of castes and subcastes in India, and these large kinship-based groups are fundamental to South Asian social structure. Each caste is part of a locally based system of interdependence with other groups, involving occupational specialization,

and is linked in complex ways with networks that stretch across regions and throughout the nation. ...

"According to the Rig Veda, sacred texts that date back to oral traditions of more than 3,000 years ago, progenitors of the four ranked varna groups sprang from various parts of the body of the primordial man, which Brahma created from clay. ... Each group had a function in sustaining the life of society—the social body. Brahmans, or priests, were created from the mouth. They were to provide for the intellectual and spiritual needs of the community. Kshatriyas, warriors and rulers, were derived from the arms. Their role was to rule and to protect others. Vaishyas—landowners and merchants—sprang from the thighs, and were entrusted with the care of commerce and agriculture. Shudras—artisans and servants—came from the feet. Their task was to perform all manual labor.

"Later conceptualized was a fifth category, 'Untouchable' menials, relegated to carrying out very menial and polluting work related to bodily decay and dirt. Since 1935 'Untouchables' have been known as Scheduled Castes, referring to their listing on government rosters, or schedules. ... Although the term Untouchable appears in literature produced by these low-ranking castes, in the 1990s, many politically conscious members of these groups prefer to refer to themselves as Dalit ..., a Hindi word meaning oppressed or downtrodden" (www.indianchild.com/caste_system_india. htm).

41. Department of Women and Child Development, "Report of the Committee on Prostitution, Child Prostitutes and Children of Prostitutes," 1998; cited in Sen, 14.

42. Asian Development Bank, 55.

43. Census of India, accessed online at www.censusindia.net/; Bureau of Democracy, Human Rights, and Labor, "Country Reports on Human Rights Practices, 2004: India."

44. Although Indian law prohibits the use of amniocentesis and sonogram tests for sex determination, family planning centers often do reveal the sex of the fetus, and the government does not effectively enforce the law prohibiting termination of a pregnancy for sexual preference.

45. Asian Development Bank, 44, slightly adapted.

46. In India, 82 percent of the people identify themselves as Hindus, while 12 percent are Muslims, and the remainder adhere to other religions or none (U.S. State Department, Bureau of Democracy, Human Rights, and Labor, "International Religious Freedom Report, 2004: India;" accessed online at www.state.gov/g/drl/rls/irf/2004/35516.htm.

47. Sen, 8.

48. Reshmi (not her real name) was rescued from a Sangli, India, brothel in a Restore International–instigated rescue operation on May 20, 2005. This information comes from a post-rescue interview with Restore International personnel.

49. Sen, 15–16; see also Sen, chapter 15.

50. UNAIDS/WHO Working Group on Global HIV/AIDS and STI Surveillance, "Epidemiological Fact Sheets on HIV/AIDS and Sexually Transmitted Infections: India," 2004; accessed online at www.data.unaids. org/Publications. See also National AIDS Control Organization, "Facts & Figures: HIV estimates, 2004;" accessed online at www.nacoonline.org/ facts_hivestimates04.htm.

51. Quoted in "India Disputes HIV Infection Claims," Agence France-Presse, April 20, 2005. Accessed online at www.aegis.com/news/ afp/2005/AF050460.html.

52. National Intelligence Council, "The Next Wave of HIV/AIDS: Nigeria, Ethiopia, Russia, India, and China," September 2002. Accessed online at www.cia.gov/nic/special_nextwaveHIV.html.

53. Avni Amin, "Risk, Morality, and Blame: A Critical Analysis of Government and U.S. Donor Responses to HIV Infections among Sex Workers in India" (Takoma Park, MD: Center for Health and Gender Equity, January 2004), 3. Accessed online at www.genderhealth.org/pubs/ AminHIVAmongSexWorkersinIndiaJan2004.pdf.

54. UNAIDS/WHO Working Group on Global HIV/AIDS and STI Surveillance, "Epidemiological Fact Sheets on HIV/AIDS and Sexually Transmitted Infections: India."

55. Sen, 95.

56. Human Rights Watch, "Future Forsaken: Abuses against Children Affected by HIV/AIDS in India," 2004, 142. Accessed online at www.hrw. org/reports/2004/india0704/FutureForsaken.pdf.

57. The Department of Women and Child Development can be accessed online at www.wcd.nic.in/. Other government bodies involved in the problem of child prostitution include the National Human Rights Commission (www.nhrc.nic.in/), the National Commission for Women (www.ncw.nic.in/home.htm), and the Central Social Welfare Board (www. cswb.org/).

58. Accessed online at www.unodc.org/unodc/trafficking_protocol. html.

59. See article 23 of the Indian Constitution. Accessed online at www.lawmin.nic.in/coi.htm.

60. See articles 366–372 of the Indian Penal Code. Accessed online at www.indialawinfo.com/bareacts/ipc.html.

61. Accessed online at www.csrindia.org.

62. Accessed online at www.vakilno1.com/bareacts/ juvenilejusticeact/juvenilejusticeact.htm.

63. U.S. State Department, Office to Monitor and Combat Trafficking in Persons, "Trafficking in Persons Report," June 2006, 137. Accessed online at www.state.gov/documents/organization/66086.pdf.

Chapter 4: A Necklace of Beads

1. Devadasi is pronounced DEE-vuh-DAH-see.

2. S. Vijaya Kumar and C. Chakrapani, *Joginism: A Bane of Indian Women* (Almora: Shri Almora Book Depot, 1993).

3. Accessed online at www.indialawinfo.com/bareacts/ipc.html.

4. Jogan Shankar, *Devadasi Cult: A Sociological Analysis* (New Delhi: Ashish, 1990); cited in Sankar Sen, ed., *Trafficking in Women and Children in India* (New Delhi: Orient Longman, 2005), 161.

5. Quoted in Usha Revelli, "Married to a Goddess," Boloji, April 24, 2005; accessed online at www.boloji.com/wfs3/wfs365.htm. Nirmala Grace is convenor of the Andhra Pradesh Anti-Jogini System Struggle Committee.

6. *United News*, slightly adapted. Accessed online at www.atruett. typepad.com/blog/2004/07/devadasis.html.

7. See Sen, chapter 13.

8. Quoted in Reuters, "Indian Cult Supplies Child Sex Trade," January 22, 1997. Accessed online at www.aegis.org/news/re/1997/ RE970188.html.

9. Nagendra Kumar Singh, *Divine Prostitution* (New Delhi: APH, 1997), 196, slightly adapted.

10. K. C. Tarachand, *Devadasi Custom: Rural Social Structure and Flesh Markets* (New Delhi: Reliance, 1991); cited in Sen, 161.

1. Singh, 212.

2. United News.

Chapter 5: A New Combatant in the War on Slavery

1. See the preface and chapter two for stories of my first encounters with slavery in India.

2. Kevin Bales, *Disposable People: New Slavery in the Global Economy* (Berkeley: University of California Press, 1999), 196.

3. *Merriam-Webster's Collegiate Dictionary*, 11th ed., under audacious.

4. See Luke 10:25-37.

5. U.S. State Department, Bureau of Democracy, Human Rights, and Labor, "International Religious Freedom Report, 2004: India." Accessed online at www.state.gov/g/drl/rls/irf/2004/35516.htm.

Chapter 6: Brothel Detectives

1. For Karishma's story, see chapter one.

2. Code of Criminal Procedure (1974), section 154. Accessed online at www.laws4india.com/acts/codeofcriminalprocedure/criminal.asp.

3. Accessed online at www.csrindia.org

4. Under Indian law, foreigners are not permitted to file a First Information Report.

Chapter 7: Going In

1. Apparently included among the underage girls picked up were one or two schoolgirls who were visiting in the area at the time and who were not involved in prostitution. We regret the inconvenience and distress they were caused, but we understand how the police could make the mistake and we are glad that the police looked into their presence in such a place.

2. Needless to say, SANGRAM/VAMP has a very different view of the rescue operation. See their perspective at www.vampnews.org/nov05/raids.html.

3. VAMP News, "About Us," www.vampnews.org/about_us.html.

4. Meena Saraswathi Seshu, "SANGRAM Accused of Interfering in the Rescue of Minor Girls," February 7, 2005; accessed online at www.ebloggy.com See also Esther Kaplan, "Pledges and Punishment," AlterNet, March 15, 2006; accessed online at www.alternet.org/rights/33284/.

5. United States Leadership against HIV/AIDS, Tuberculosis, and Malaria Act of 2003, accessed online at www.frwebgate.access.gpo.gov/cgi-bin

6. U.S. Agency for International Development, "Trafficking in Persons: The USAID Strategy for Response," February 2003, 4. Accessed online at www.usaid.gov/our_work/cross-cutting_programs/wid/pubs/pd-abx-358-final.pdf.

7. Accessed online at www.genderhealth.org/pubs/20050518LTR.pdf.

8. The letter is dated October 6, 2005; accessed online at www.souder.house.gov/UploadedFiles/20051006CongressmanSouderUSAIDLetter.pdf. Because of the hidden funding through AVERT, a bill was introduced in the 109th Congress to require full disclosure of all entities and organizations receiving federal funds.

9. Quoted in Representative Souder's letter to James Kunder.

10. Quoted in Rema Nagarajan, "US Accuses NGO of 'Trafficking,'" *Hindustan Times*, September 29, 2005. Accessed online at www.hindustantimes.com/news/181_1504660,00050001.htm.

11. Letter to James Kunder.

12. Accessed online at www.thomas.loc.gov/cgi-bin/query/F?r109:29:./temp/~r109GddDdy:e253814:.

13. Accessed online at www.frwebgate.access.gpo.gov/cgi-bin/getdoc.cgi?dbname=109_cong_public_laws&docid=f:publ282.109.pdf.

14. Unfortunately, these police-only raids are not above criticism. According to a government report, some police forces will schedule a brothel raid merely to make their record look better or as a punishment against brothel keepers who have stopped paying bribes to the police. Also, sometimes the police will arrest prostitutes and not brothel keepers, in effect punishing the victims and letting the perpetrators go free (Sankar Sen, *Trafficking in Women and Children in India* [New Delhi: Orient Longman, 2005], 110–11). For all these reasons, it is invaluable for members of an NGO to accompany police on a raid.

15. "Rescued from Prostitution, a Fresh Beginning," Express News Service, May 7, 2004. Accessed online at www.cities.expressindia.com/fullstory.php?newsid=83969.

16. One government study of brothels stated, "In the absence of any intervention by law enforcement agencies, the owners continued to exploit the trafficked victims with impunity" (Sen, 110).

Chapter 8: Putting the Bad Guys behind Bars

1. In India, any citizen can fill out an FIR reporting a crime. But the police are not required to charge-sheet the crime; they can just ignore the FIR if they want. That's why we have to provide strong evidence of a crime being committed when we try to get police action against the brothel keepers of minor girls—it puts pressure on them to act. In this case, though, we had negotiated for the full cooperation of the police before the raid was even carried out. There was little doubt that they would charge-sheet it.

2. Immoral Trafficking (Prevention) Act, section 7. Accessed online at www.csrindia.org

3. Ibid., sections 3–6.

4. Ibid., sections 7–8.

5. Research has shown that in many cases, following a rescue operation, police have taken the brothel keepers' word for the age of the prostitutes, resulting in rapid retrafficking of the girls into brothels (Sankar Sen, ed., *The Trafficking of Women and Children in India* [New Delhi: Orient Longman, 2005], 202). That's one reason why it is so important for members of an NGO like Restore International to be present during the legal proceedings and ensure that the girls are properly taken care of.

6. Ibid., 563.

7. Article 23 of the Constitution of India; accessed online at www.lawmin.nic.in/coi.htm. See also articles 15, 21, 24, 51.

8. See articles 366–372 of the Indian Penal Code. Accessed online at www.indialawinfo.com/bareacts/ipc.html.

9. Accessed online at www.csrindia.org

10. Sen, 199.

11. See sections 41 and 44 of the Juvenile Justice Act. Accessed online at www.vakilno1.com/bareacts/juvenilejusticeact/juvenilejusticeact.htm.

12. Sen, 205.

13. Sadly, while India has adequate laws against sex trafficking, most trafficking victims don't know they exist. In one survey of a large number of girls and women who had been rescued from brothels, 88.4 percent said they were not aware of any law against trafficking and 79.7 percent said they did not know of any law prohibiting sexual abuse or exploitation of children (ibid., 75).

14. Sen, 197–8.

15. Ibid., 200.

16. Ibid., 203.

17. Ibid., 19.

18. Ibid., 20.

19. Committee on Prostitution, Child Prostitutes and Children of Prostitutes, Department of Women and Child Development, "Plan of Action to Combat Trafficking and Commercial Sexual Exploitation of Women and Children," 1998. Accessed online at www.ecpat-esp.org/documentacion/planes-nacionales/India.pdf.

20. Sen, 211.

Chapter 9: The Chance for a New Life

1. Unclassified U.S. State Department memorandum "Reported Trafficking Complicity of USAID-funded Indian NGO 'SANGRAM,' " August 22, 2005, cited in letter from Congressman Mark E. Souder to James Kunder, assistant administrator with USAID; accessed online at www.souder.house.gov/UploadedFiles/20051006CongressmanSouderUSAIDLetter.pdf.

2. Due to errors made at this time, the chairperson of the Sangli Child Welfare Committee was removed and replaced by someone else.

3. We filed a complaint in court, and we tried tracking down the missing girls, but once they scattered, it became difficult to find them. In fact, it was while trying to find one of these retrafficked girls in Sangli that we suffered the mob attack described at the beginning of chapter five.

4. Kevin Bales, *Understanding Global Slavery: A Reader* (Berkeley: University of California Press, 2005), 67.

5. The Juvenile Justice Act is available online at www.vakilno1.com/bareacts/juvenilejusticeact/juvenilejusticeact.htm (see especially sections 9 and 12). For the Department of Women and Child Development, see online at www.wcd.nic.in/. The status of state-by-state implementation of the Juvenile Justice Act is tracked online at www.socialjustice.nic.in/social/impleJJ.htm.

6. Office to Monitor and Combat Trafficking in Persons, "How Can I Recognize Victims of Trafficking?" July 28, 2004. Accessed online at www.state.gov/g/tip/rls/fs/34563.htm.

7. "These government run homes have been criticised for a host of shortcomings—corruption, poor infrastructure facilities, meager budgets, inadequate provisions for psychological care, ineffective skill building etc. ... Most women end up doing nothing for long periods in these homes, while those who do not wish to be rescued, view the home as a prison" (Sankar Sen, ed., *The Trafficking of Women and Children in India* [New Delhi: Orient Longman, 2005], 21).

8. Ibid., 79.

9. In a survey of rescued girls, 16 percent had stayed in a government rescue home for less than a month, 13 percent had stayed there for from one to five months, 10 percent had stayed there for from five months to a year, and 24 percent had stayed there for more than a year. (The rest did not respond to the question.) The maximum period any respondent had stayed at such a home was two years (ibid.).

10. This is the case for girls who have been trafficked within India. The situation can be much worse for girls trafficked from foreign nations such as Nepal and Bangladesh, since India has no laws governing repatriation of foreign women and girls. Sometimes these females are stuck at the border or languish in rehab homes (ibid., 22).

11. A government-funded study concluded about rescued girls, "Social stigma is the greatest obstacle to reintegration." And when the girls can't go home and don't have any marketable skills, they tend to drift back into prostitution (ibid., 21).

12. Sen, 83.

13. Robert I. Friedman, "India's Shame: Sexual Slavery and Political Corruption Are Leading to an AIDS Catastrophe," *The Nation*, April 8, 1996, 20.

14. Sen, 80.

15. Asian Development Bank, "Combating Trafficking of Women and Children in South Asia: Regional Synthesis Paper for Bangladesh, India, and Nepal," April 2003, 44. Accessed online at www.adb.org/Documents/ Books/Combating_Trafficking/default.asp.

Chapter 10: From Here—Where?

1. For more on Snekithar, see www.indiaexportcompany.com. The term snekithar sounds something like "snaky dar."

2. Quoted in José Luis Alcázar, "Childhood in the Pits," Inter Press Service News Agency, October 4, 2005. Accessed online at www.ipsnews. net/news.asp?idnews=30525.

3. An award-winning documentary called *The Devil's Miner* follows the lives of two young brothers working a mine in Bolivia (www. thedevilsminer.com/).

4. U.S. State Department, Bureau of Democracy, Human Rights, and Labor, "Country Reports on Human Rights Practices: Uganda," 2005 (released March 8, 2006). Accessed online at www.state.gov/g/drl/rls/ hrrpt/2005/61598.htm.

5. CIA, "The World Factbook: Refugees and Internally Displaced Persons." Accessed online at www.cia.gov/cia/publications/factbook/fields/2194.html.

Chapter 11: Toward a Modern Abolition Movement

1. For Anti-Slavery International, see www.antislavery.org/. The organization's U.S. counterpart is Free the Slaves (www.freetheslaves.net/).

2. Kevin Bales, *Understanding Global Slavery: A Reader* (Berkeley: University of California Press, 2005), 125.

3. For example, the Congressional Research Service has issued a report summarizing the history of the United States's response to trafficking in women and children. The report identifies certain outstanding questions about the implementation of current U.S. policy, such as "How will the war on terrorism and the emphasis on homeland security affect the efforts to combat human trafficking" and "Should sanctions against foreign governments be used as a policy instrument to combat trafficking?" (Francis T. Miko, "Trafficking in Women and Children: The U.S. and International Response," [Congressional Research Service, updated March 26, 2004]; accessed online at www.fpc.state.gov/documents/organization/31990.pdf). On an international level, the International Labour Organization, in its report "A Global Alliance against Forced Labour," included an action plan to combat forced labor. This plan calls for (among other things) improved legislation, better rehabilitation programs, and outreach to workers' groups (International Labour Organization, "A Global Alliance against Forced Labour: Global Report under the Follow-up to the ILO Declaration on Fundamental Principles and Rights at Work," 82–87; accessed online atwww.ilo.org/dyn/declaris/DECLARATIONWEB.DOWNLOAD_BLOB?Var_DocumentID=5059). Furthermore, a body of governmental and nongovernmental experts on human trafficking issued the Miami Declaration of Principles on Human Trafficking on February 10, 2005. These broad-based principles call upon nation-states to strengthen their anti-trafficking laws, fight internal corruption, improve trafficking prosecution, review their immigration policies, protect trafficking victims, cooperate with NGOs, and much more ("The Miami Declaration of Principles on Human Trafficking," February 10, 2005; accessed online at www.humantrafficking.org/countries/eap/united_states/news/2005_04/miami_declaration.html).

4. The human rights organization Rugmark provides one model for attacking the economic underpinnings of child exploitation (www. rugmark.org/). This organization recruits carpet producers and importers in India and neighboring countries to make and sell carpets that are free of illegal child labor. By agreeing to adhere to Rugmark's strict no-child-labor guidelines, and by permitting random inspections of carpet looms, manufacturers receive the right to put the Rugmark label on their carpets. The label provides the best possible assurance to consumers that children were not employed in the making of a rug. It also verifies that a portion of the carpet price is contributed to the rehabilitation and education of former child weavers.

5. Go to www.google.com/alerts.

6. Go to www.restoreinternational.org.

7. To find out how to contact your elected officials, go to www. congress.org/stickers/?dir=congressorg&officials=1.

8. To search for job opportunities at Restore International, go to www.restoreinternational.org.

9. To learn more about Restore International vision trips, go to www. restoreinternational.org.

10. To learn how to book a Restore International speaker, go to www. restoreinternational.org.

11. To learn how to contribute to Restore International work, go to www.indiaexportcompany.com and www.restoreinternational.org.

Appendix: Legal Instruments Related to Modern-Day Slavery

1. Many of these instruments are treated in depth in *United Nations, Economic and Social Commission for Asia and the Pacific, Combating Human Trafficking in Asia: A Resource Guide to International and Regional Legal Instruments, Political Commitments and Recommended Practices* (New York: United Nations, 2003); accessed online at www.unescap.org/esid/Gad/Publication/Trafficking-File1.pdf and www.unescap.org/esid/Gad/Publication/Trafficking-File2.pdf. See also Sankar Sen, ed., *Trafficking in Women and Children in India* (New Delhi: Orient Longman, 2005), chapter 16; accessed online at www.ashanet.org/focusgroups/sanctuary/articles/ReportonTrafficking.pdf.

GLOSSARY
OF ACRONYMS

ARTWAC — Action Research on Trafficking in Women and Women
ASEM — Asia Europe Meeting
CRC — Convention on the Rights of the Child
CSWB— Central Social Welfare Board (India)
CWC — Child Welfare Committee (India)
CSE — commercial sexual exploitation
DWCD — Department of Women and Child Development (India)
ECPAT — End Child Prostitution, Child Pornography and Trafficking
of Children for Sexual Purposes
HIV/AIDS — Human Immuno-deficiency Virus/Acquired Immune
Deficiency Syndrome
IDP — internally displaced person
ILO — International Labor Organization
IOM — International Organization for Migration
IPC — Indian Penal Code
IPEC — International Program for the Elimination of
Child Labor (ILO)
ITPA — Immoral Trafficking (Protection) Act (India)
JJA — Juvenile Justice Act (India)
LRA — Lord's Resistance Army (Uganda)
NCW — National Commission for Women (India)

NGO — nongovernmental organization
NHRC — National Human Rights Commission
OHCHR — Office of the High Commissioner for
Human Rights (UN)
SAARC — South Asian Association for Regional Cooperation
SANGRAM — Sampada Grameen Mahila Sanstha
STD — sexually transmitted disease
TVPA — Trafficking Victims Protection Act (US)
TVPRA — Trafficking Victims Protection Reauthorization Act (US)
UN — United Nations
UNICEF — United Nations Children's Fund
USAID — United States Agency for International Development
VAMP — Veshya AIDS Muqabla Parishad
WHO — World Health Organization

INDEX

A

B

number of children in, 78
parents' motivations and, 79–80
prostitution and, 83–85
victim profiles of, 56–57, 62–64, 68–69, 75–76
DeWalt, Danny, 11
Digrej, India, 25
Doddridge, Philip, 163
Domestic slavery, 34, 44
Dorsey, Ilea, 158
Dowries, 65–66

E
Egeland, Jan, 157
Emancipation Act (Great Britain), 35, 164
Emancipation Proclamation (U.S.), 35
Eunuchs, 54, 106

F
Falkland Road, Mumbai, India, 54, 57, 148
Fatalism, 67
FBI, 41
Feachem, Richard, 70
Foreign Contribution Regulation Act (India), 98
Foreigners Act (India), 98
France, 35
Freedom Firm, 171
Friedman, Robert I., 57–58

G
Goa, India, 54
Gokul Nagar district, Sangli, India, 20, 62–64, 89–92, 101–3, 111–12, 115–16, 117–20, 129–31, 143
Gollar, Bhimavva Durgappa, 120
Gray, Simon, 36
Great Britain, 35, 163–64
Gulu, Uganda, 159
Gupta, Vinod, 124

following example of, 10, 27, 32, 73, 98, 153, 159, 169
 lost sheep parable of, 28
Juvenile Justice (Care and Protection of Children) Act (India), 134, 135,
 136, 145

K

Kamla, Sarthak, 129
Kampala, Uganda, 150, 158, 159
Karishma
 background of, 25–26
 discovery of, 17–23, 171
 attempted rescue of, 24–25, 26
 disappearance of, 26–28, 171
 rediscovery of, 171–72
 freedom for, 172
 future for, 172
 photos of, 19, 27
Karma, 67
Karnataka, India, 96
Karnataka Devadasis Act, 78
Kolhapur, India, 25, 26, 62, 106–07, 139
Koli, Padma Hanmant, 120
Kony, Joseph, 157
Kovalam, India, 54
Kumar (bonded laborer), 154–55
Kunder, James, 121

L

Labor, forced. *See* Slavery
League of Nations, 35, 175
Lebanon, 34
Legislators, writing to, 168
Lincoln, Abraham, 35
Lord's Resistance Army, 157–58

M

Madras Devadasi Prevention of Dedication Act, 78
Maharashtra, India, 84, 96
Mahbubnagar, India, 82
Mammallpuram, India, 54

T

Tamil Nadu, India, 29, 47, 54, 96, 154–55
Thasildar, Mehboob, 57
Theosophical Society of India, 77
Tio, 156
Trafficking Victims Protection Act (U.S.), 38, 136
Trafficking Victims Protection Reauthorization Act (U.S.), 136
Truong, Thanh-Dam, 43
Tubman, Harriet, 127

U

Uganda, 141, 147, 157–60
Underground Railroad, 127
UNICEF, 45
United Nations, 35–36, 93, 137–38, 175–76
United States
  funding from, 120–24
  slavery in, 35, 38, 165
  trafficking laws of, 136
Universal Declaration of Human Rights, 35, 175
U.S. State Department, 37, 38–39, 72, 93
USAID, 120–22

V

VAMP, 119–24, 131
Victim profiles. *See also* Karishma
  Anahita (devadasi), 62–64
  Darja (forced prostitute), 89–90, 113–16
  Kumar (bonded laborer), 154–55
  Mary (child soldier), 46
  Neary (forced prostitute), 47
  Reshmi (devadasi), 68–69
  Sattyava (devadasi), 75–76
  Silvia (domestic slave), 34
  Yauvani (devadasi), 56–57
Vidyasagar, Isvar Chandra, 77
Vision trips, 168